Creating Heirloom Teddy Bears

THE COMPLETE PATTERN BOOK

By Linda Mullins
Illustrated by Gisele Nash

Published By **Hobby House Press, Inc.**

DEDICATION
This book is affectionately dedicated to my friend Georgi Bohrod Rothe.

ACKNOWLEDGMENT
My sincere thanks and appreciation goes out to six dear friends and business associates that worked with me on this book. Their enthusiasm, willing support and invaluable suggestions made this project an enjoyable reality for me: Teddy Bear artist Flore Emory; artist Gisele Nash, consultant Georgi Bohrod Rothe, my patient and well-advising editor Mary Beth Ruddell, and finally my wonderful publishers Gary and Mary Ruddell.

Front Cover
Left: Mitchom. Ideal Bear Circa 1907. 18in (46cm); short gold mohair; shoe button eyes; jointed arms and legs; swivel head; excelsior stuffing. **Right:** Mitchom. Bear. 1994. 18in (46cm); short gold mohair; shoe button eyes; jointed arms and legs; swivel head; polyester fiberfill stuffing. Rendition of the 1907 Ideal Bear on the left.

Published by  Hobby House Press, Inc.
Grantsville, Maryland 21536

Additional copies of this book may be purchased at $24.95
(plus postage and handling) from
Hobby House Press, Inc.
1 Corporate Drive
Grantsville, Maryland 21536
1-800-554-1447
or from your favorite bookstore or dealer.

©1995 Linda Mullins
All rights reserved. No part of this book may be reproduced or utilized in any form or by any means, electronic or mechanical, including photocopying, recording, or by any information storage and retrieval system, without permission in writing from the publisher. Inquiries should be addressed to:
Hobby House Press, Inc., 1 Corporate Drive, Grantsville, Maryland 21536.
Printed in the United States of America
ISBN: 0-87588-444-X

Table of Contents

9 Hangtags...Personalize Your Heirloom

Introduction 4
The Roosevelt Bear 5
Mitchom – America's First Teddy Bear 6
Liberty – An Early American Teddy Bear 7
Baron and Rolph – Early German Teddy Bears 8
Crämer the Clown 9
Musical Jopi 10
Churchill and Chad – Early British Bears 11
Portrait of a Teddy Bear Artist – Flore Emory 12

Let's Make A Bear (Instructions)

Roosevelt 14
Mitchom 16
Liberty 18
Baron 20
Rolph 22
Crämer the Clown 24
Musical Jopi 26
Churchill 28
Chad 30
Basic Hints 32
Tools and Fabrics 35
Dyeing 36

Patterns For Making Linda's Bears

Roosevelt 56
Mitchom 59
Liberty 64
Baron 68
Rolph 70
Crämer the Clown 72
Musical Jopi 77
Churchill 82
Chad 86

INTRODUCTION

Teddy bears were born in the early days of the 20th Century. Actually, the bear itself has been a favorite with children and adults since the 19th Century and ancient cultures revered its powers as both magical and holy.

The Steiff Company is most often credited with creating the teddy bear as we know it today. But the name "Teddy" came from President Theodore Roosevelt.

As the popularity of teddy bears has skyrocketed among collectors, original antique bears have become expensive and difficult to find.

Both collectors undying search for historical bears and artist's appreciation and respect of early teddy bears inspired me to put this book together. These wonderful renditions of memorable bears of the past would otherwise be inaccessible to the average collector.

All the bears in the book come from my private collection. I selected a variety of some of my most favorite bears. As you can see, each bear has definite identifiable characteristics which can be attributed to either a specific manufacturer or a country of origin.

Renowned teddy bear artist Flore Emory is an expert at recreating early bear designs without dismantling the original models. Her expertise made it possible to bring you nine rendition patterns of my special antique bears.

I commissioned talented artist Gisele Nash, creator of the Cinnabears by Gund, to do the artwork and layout for this book. Her attractive, clear, simple, step-by-step illustrations will insure a fun, interesting and successful bear making project.

In addition, numerous bear making tips will further aid you in creating these bears, or any bears you may produce in the future.

As always, historical information will enhance your interest and love of each bear.

I hope you enjoy your bear making experience as much as I enjoy sharing these special bears with you!

The ROOSEVELT Bear

This dear little American-made bear proudly tells about the man with whom he shares his name — President Theodore Roosevelt. A hero to millions of Americans, "Teddy" Roosevelt's love of nature, children and animals is legendary. He was first elected to the presidency in 1901 and went on to become one of the most popular of all U.S. Chief Executives.

Although he is remembered as a great hunter, Roosevelt's passion for hunting bears was not solely to kill them, but to observe their natural habits. Grizzly bears became his favorites. In what is now a legendary story, the teddy bear got his name from this kind, gallant president.

On a hunting trip back in 1902, Roosevelt just didn't have the heart to shoot a poor old bear cornered by his hunting party. When the story got out, predominantly from a famous cartoon drawn by Clifford Berryman and published in *The Washington Post*, manufacturers started making toy bears. This coincided with an influx of stuffed, mohair bruins from Europe. Every one started calling these bears "Teddy" after the president who, it was said, "grew up to be the man of his youthful dreams."

MITCHOM
America's First Teddy Bear

There are many who would say that this appealing bear was indeed a representation of one of the very first teddy bears produced in our country. Legend has it that in 1902, the founder of The Ideal Toy Company (Morris Mitchom) saw the now-famous Clifford Berryman cartoon of President Roosevelt's encounter with a bear. He was inspired. His wife hand-stitched a lovable, jointed bear who was displayed in the window of their small shop in Brooklyn, New York.

It is said that Mitchom then wrote to Teddy Roosevelt to elicit his permission to name the animal "Teddy." The President congenially acquiesced.

The Mitchom "Mom and Pop" operation grew to be a large conglomerate over the years. When the Butler Brothers backed Mitchom's credit with plush producing mills the Ideal Novelty Toy Company was born. (In 1938 the name was shortened to the Ideal Toy Company.) Eventually, Ideal became an indirect wholly-owned subsidiary of Tyco Toys.

Mitchom Bear (page 16) embodies the endearing physical early Ideal characteristics that are still favored among teddy bear lovers. Look at his wide triangular head, large, widely set ears, arms positioned low on his shoulders, pads on the feet coming to a point, short mohair and fairly long and slender body.

LIBERTY
An Early American Teddy Bear

By 1907, teddy bear factories opened up in almost every major city throughout the United States. More than 20 companies were making teddy bears in the U.S. alone. Even though the teddy bear was a toy that enchanted children, the spell of the cuddly new toy was quick to bewitch adults as well. Never before had anything compared to the teddy bear craze.

Unfortunately, there were a great number of American bears that were not identified with any permanent manufacturer's mark. Nor have any advertisements surfaced to aid us in the identification of "mystery" bears.

Liberty (page 18) is one of these many mystery bears. He could have been made by any one of a plethora of American bear manufacturers. This charming bear portrays the characteristics more commonly used in early American bears – a roundish head, large round ears positioned low on the head and eyes sewn close together.

BARON AND ROLPH
Early German Bears

As long ago as the 16th Century, the doll and plush industry had its roots in a lush valley near Sonneberg, Germany. Two miles due east from Neustadt, Sonneberg became known as the "cradle of dolls, teddy bears and plush animals." Although that was the heart of the German toy industry, teddy bears were also produced in Nurnberg. However, the most famous teddy bear manufacturer of all time had its headquarters approximately 200 miles from the Sonneberg-Neustadt region. Steiff began to produce teddy bears in 1903. At that time, the teddy bear was relatively unknown to the many plush toy producers in the Sonnenberg-Neustadt region.

It is said that it was an American businessman who asked one of Neustadt's largest plush manufacturers to produce teddies for the American market. Soon business was booming. Even ten year old children worked 10-12 hours a day, along side of their parents and other family members. In the years from 1908 to 1914, at least 2,000 to 3,000 teddy bears were made daily, and up to 90% of them shipped to the U.S.

Baron (page 20) and Rolph (page 22) are examples of these beautiful bears from Germany. Today many German children grow up with those wonderful friends their ancestors helped create – the German Teddy Bear.

CRÄMER The Clown

The first Crämer teddy bears were surrounded by controversy. The press claimed that Crämer was using Steiff's patterns. Once this problem was corrected, Crämer began creating unique looking bears of their own.

The company, run by Eduard Crämer and his wife Anna, mainly produced animals from 1896 to 1906 in the little German village of Schalkau in the Thüringen area close to Sonneberg. In 1896 Edward Crämer registered the name "EDUCA" as its trademark along with the drawing of the head of the monkey.

In the 1920s, bears made of mohair and wool plush were introduced. This gave a more wild and rough look to the toy bruins. Sometimes Crämer employed ribbon ruffles, pom-poms and pointed hats which gave their bears a clown-like appearance.

Also introduced in the 1920s were walking and musical bears. A complicated musical mechanism was advertised by Crämer in 1930. Exquisitely sweet music was produced when the head of the bear was tilted back and forth.

Our Crämer the Clown (page 24) represents one of these rare and unique creations of the past. He is made of long, silky, pinkish mohair. His shield-shaped, shaved snout and deep, pink, buttonhole stitched smiling mouth (a Crämer characteristic) make him look very alert and friendly. Still wearing his original silk ribbon ruff, pom-poms and felt-pointed clown hat, he smugly smiles knowing when he is affectionately held, a secretly concealed music box will ring out, surprising his new friend.

Musical JOPI

After 1925, following a decade of war, crisis and stringency, novelties once again were on the forefront of toy production. Probably the most imaginative, original, charming and enduring of these designs was the musical teddy bear. Around 1930, concertina squeeze-box type music boxes concealed in the torso of the bear were produced by the German company, Jopi. Possessing all the charm of a teddy bear and perfectly constructed of soft, silky bear skin, the Jopi bear also offered beautiful music at the whim of his owner. To play lovely melodies, all one had to do was hold teddy around his tummy with both hands and gently squeeze.

The art of adding a different color to the tip of the mohair by hand first was popularized in the 1920s. Our Jopi bear (page 26) is proud to have been produced in a vivid green tipped mohair.

Another precious characteristic of Jopi bears are their big, kind eyes. All these appealing traits are sure to steal your heart even today.

CHURCHILL AND CHAD
EARLY BRITISH BEARS

The increased popularity of bears in the early 1900s induced the English toy makers to create their own version of the teddy bear. They had all the basic requirements for teddy bear making right in their own back yard. Even the mohair plush for making bearskins was made just north of London.

Identification of early English bears is difficult because so many were unmarked. Churchill (page 28) is one of these unmarked bears, but never the less proud to be a British bear. He represents the slightly plump torso, short arms and clear glass eyes — characteristics of this era.

Churchill's companion, Chad, (page 30) was made by Chad Valley, a leading toy maker in England founded in 1823. By 1920, Chad Valley specialized in bear making. Fortunately for collectors, Chad Valley was one of the few companies that labeled their toys. Prior to 1930, a woven label appeared on the foot. They also implanted a metal button with the words "Chad Valley English Hygienic Toys." Chad represents a rarely found, special trait of Chad Valley bears: He is made of bright fuschia-colored plush and still has the manufacturers' button in his ear and label on his

PORTRAIT OF A TEDDY BEAR ARTIST
FLORE EMORY

After an unsuccessful attempt to repair a badly damaged antique bear from her own collection, Flore Emory decided to try her hand at creating a new bear on her own. That was 1979. Now Flore sells her hand-crafted creations to collectors all over the world. Flore and I have worked together on various bear-related projects for more than a decade. She has indeed made each project especially fun with her warm personality and captivating creativity. Flore has once again done an excellent job. Even though she did not dismantle any of my favorite bears to draw her patterns, she has captured the individual special look which faithfully replicates each antique design and gives each bear its individual character.

Let's Make A Bear

ROOSEVELT
Unidentified American manufacturer. Circa 1907.
13in (33cm).

ROOSEVELT

Materials

You will need a piece of mohair or synthetic plush 56in (142cm) wide by 12in (31cm) long.
The fur should be 1/4in (.65cm) in length.
Tools. Please refer to page 35

16in (41cm) by 4in (10cm) wool felt for pads
4 1-3/4in (5cm) fiberboard disks for arms
4 1-3/4in (5cm) fiberboard disks for legs
2 2-1/2in (6cm) fiberboard disks for neck
10 metal washers
5 metal cotter pins
2 8mm black shoe-button type eyes
Polyester fiberfill for stuffing
Black pearl cotton for nose, mouth and claws
Button/Carpet thread for closing seams and affixing ears and eyes
Basic Hints. Please refer to pages 32, 33 and 34.

Roosevelt is 13in (33cm) tall.

Pattern layout for Roosevelt

▦ Indicates pattern to be placed with printed side down.

Step One:

1. Mount pattern onto sturdy material
   i.e. card board and cut out.
2. Trace pattern onto fabric backing using permanent marker and following layout shown on this page. Make sure arrows go in the same direction as nap.
3. Transfer all markings.
4. Cut out taking care to cut fabric backing and not fur on the other side.

Step Two: Sewing (pages 38-39)
Step Three: Head, Eyes and Ears (pages 40-41)
Step Four: Nose and Mouth (page 42)
Step Five: Assembly (pages 46-47)
Step Six: Finishing (pages 48-49)

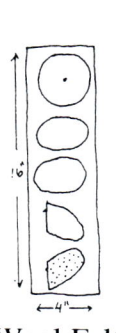

Wool Felt

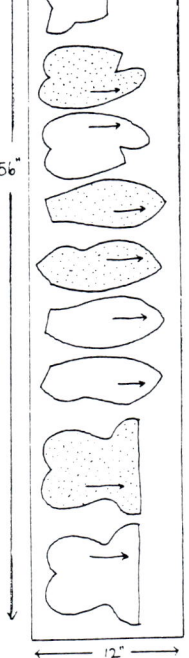

MITCHOM
Ideal. Circa 1907.
18in (46cm).

MITCHOM
The First American Teddy Bear

Materials
You will need a piece of mohair or synthetic plush 56in (142cm) wide by 30in (76cm) long. The fur should be 1/4in (.65cm) in length.
Tools. Please refer to page 35.

20in (51cm) by 8in (20cm) wool felt for pads
8in (20cm) by 8in (20cm) piece of stiff cardboard
4 1-3/4in (5cm) fiberboard disks for arms
4 2-1/2in (6cm) fiberboard disks for legs
2 2-1/2in (6cm) fiberboard disks for neck
10 metal washers
5 metal cotter pins
2 14mm black glass eyes
Polyester fiberfill for stuffing
Black pearl cotton for nose, mouth and claws.
Button/Carpet thread for closing seams and affixing ears and eyes
Basic Hints. Please refer to pages 32, 33 and 34.

***Mitchom** is 18in (46cm) tall.*

Pattern layout for Mitchom

Indicates pattern to be placed with printed side down.

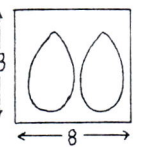

Cardboard

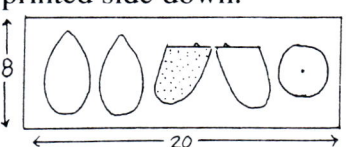

Wool Felt

Step One:
1. Mount pattern onto sturdy material *i.e. cardboard* and cut out.
2. Trace pattern onto fabric backing using permanent marker and following layout shown on this page. Make sure arrows go in the same direction as nap.
3. Transfer all markings.
4. Cut out taking care to cut fabric backing and not fur on the other side.

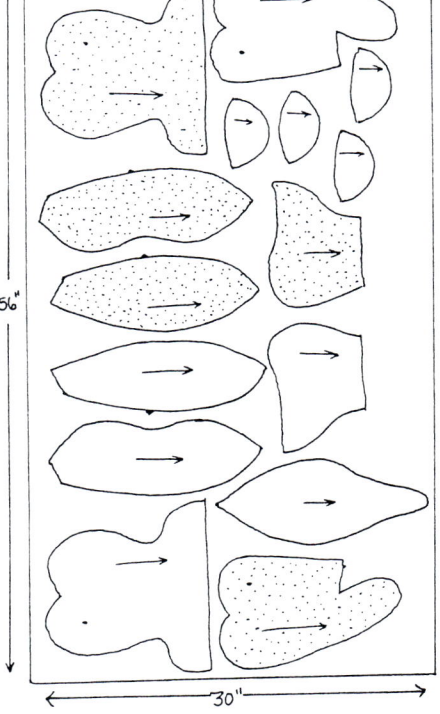

Step Two: Sewing (pages 38-39)
Step Three: Head, Eyes and Ears (pages 40-41)
Step Four: Nose and Mouth
(page 42)
Step Five: Assembly
(pages 46-47)
Step Six: Finishing
(pages 48-49)

LIBERTY
Unidentified American manufacturer. Circa 1907.
16in (41cm).

LIBERTY
An Early American Teddy Bear

Liberty is 16in (41cm) tall.

Materials

You will need a piece of mohair or synthetic plush 56in (142cm) wide by 18in (46cm) long. The fur should be 1/2in (1cm) in length.
Tools. Please refer to page 35.

16in (41cm) by 5in (13cm) wool felt for pads
4 1-3/4in (5cm) fiberboard disks for arms
4 1-3/4in (5cm) fiberboard disks for legs
2 2-1/2in (6cm) fiberboard disks for neck
10 metal washers
5 metal cotter pins
2 10mm shoe button-type eyes
Polyester fiberfill for stuffing
Rust colored pearl cotton for nose, mouth and claws
Button/Carpet thread for closing seams and affixing eyes and ears
Basic Hints. Please refer to pages 32, 33 and 34.

Pattern layout for Liberty

▦ Indicates pattern to be placed with printed side down.

Wool Felt

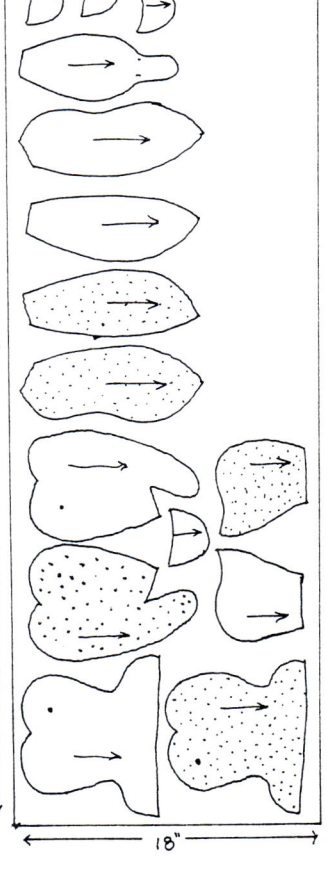

Step One:
1. Mount pattern onto sturdy material *i.e.* cardboard and cut out.
2. Trace pattern onto fabric backing using permanent marker and following layout shown on this page. Make sure arrows go in the same direction as nap.
3. Transfer all markings.
4. Cut out taking care to cut fabric backing and not fur on the other side.

Step Two: Sewing (pages 38-39)
Step Three: Head, Eyes and Ears
(pages 40-41)
Step Four: Nose and Mouth
(page 43)
Step Five: Assembly
(pages 46-47)
Step Six: Finishing
(pages 48-49)

BARON
Unidentified German manufacturer. Circa 1907.
10in (25cm).

BARON
An Early German Bear

Materials

You will need a piece of mohair or synthetic plush 30in (76cm) wide by 8in (20cm) long.
The fur should be 1/4in (.65cm) in length.
Tools. Please refer to page 35.

6in (15cm) by 6in (15cm) wool felt for pads
4 1-1/4in (3cm) fiberboard disks for arms
4 1-1/4in (3cm) fiberboard disks for legs
2 1-1/2in (4cm) fiberboard disks for neck
10 metal washers
5 metal cotter pins
2 6mm black shoe button-type eyes
Polyester fiberfill for stuffing
Black pearl cotton for nose, mouth and claws
Button/Carpet thread for closing seams and affixing ears and eyes
Basic Hints. Please refer to pages 32, 33 and 34.

***Baron** is 10in (25cm) tall.*

Pattern layout for Baron

 Indicates pattern to be placed with printed side down.

Step One:

1. Mount pattern onto sturdy material *i.e. cardboard and cut out.*
2. Trace pattern onto fabric backing using permanent marker and following layout shown on this page. Make sure arrows go in the same direction as nap.
3. Transfer all markings.
4. Cut out taking care to cut fabric backing and not fur on the other side.

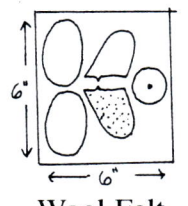
Wool Felt

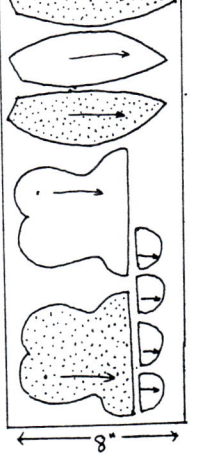

Step Two: Sewing (pages 38-39)
Step Three: Head, Eyes and Ears
(pages 40-41)
Step Four: Nose and Mouth
(page 43)
Step Five: Assembly (pages 46-47)
Step Six: Finishing (pages 48-49)

ROLPH
Unidentified German manufacturer. Circa 1907.
9in (23cm) long and 5-1/2in (14cm) tall.

ROLPH
AN EARLY GERMAN BEAR

Materials
You will need a piece of mohair or synthetic plush 34in (86cm) wide by 10in (25cm) long.
The fur should be 1/4in (.65cm) in length.
Tools. Please refer to page 35.

5in (13cm) by 4in (10cm) wool felt for pads
8 1in (3cm) fiberboard disks for legs
8 metal washers
4 metal cotter pins
2 6mm black shoe-button type eyes
Polyester fiberfill for stuffing
Black pearl cotton for nose and mouth
Button/Carpet thread for closing seams and affixing ears and eyes
Basic Hints. Please refer to pages 32, 33 and 34.

Rolph is 9in (23cm) long and 5-1/2in (14cm) tall.

Pattern layout for Rolph

Indicates pattern to be placed with printed side down.

Step One:
1. Mount pattern onto sturdy material
   i.e. cardboard and cut out.
2. Trace pattern onto fabric backing using permanent marker and following layout shown on this page. Make sure arrows go in the same direction as nap.
3. Transfer all markings.
4. Cut out taking care to cut fabric backing and not fur on the other side.

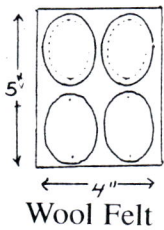
Wool Felt

Step Two: Sewing Rolph (pages 50-51)
Step Three: Assembling Rolph (page 52)
Step Four: Rolph's Headwork (page 53)
Step Five: Finishing Rolph
(page 54)

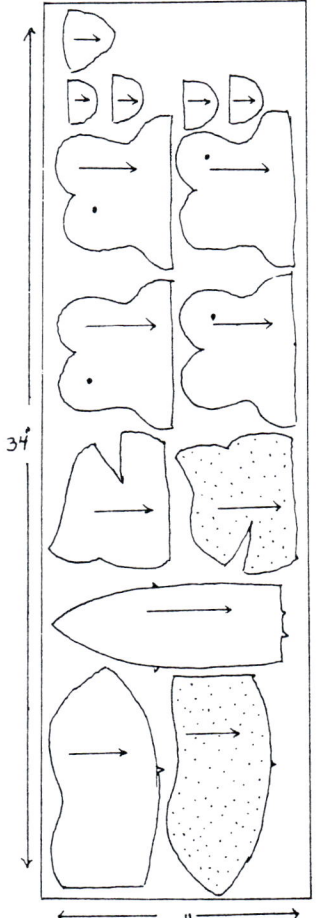

CRÄMER the Clown
Circa 1930. 16in (41cm).

CRÄMER the Clown

Materials

You will need a piece of mohair or synthetic plush 56in (142cm) wide by 24in (61cm) long. The fur should be 3/4in (7cm) in length.

Tools. Please refer to page 35.

15in (38cm) by 9in (23cm) wool felt for pads
4 2in (5cm) fiberboard disks for arms
4 2-1/2in (6cm) fiberboard disks for legs
2 2-1/2in (6cm) fiberboard disks for neck
10 metal washers
5 metal cotter pins
2 12mm amber glass eyes
Polyester fiberfill for stuffing
Brown pearl cotton for nose and claws
Pink pearl cotton for mouth
Button/Carpet thread for closing seams and affixing ears and eyes
9in (23cm) by 5in (13cm) wool felt for hat
9in (23cm) by 5in (13cm) contrasting wool felt for hat
1-1/2yd (137cm) of 1-1/2in (4cm) wide ribbon
3 pom-poms

Basic Hints. Please refer to pages 32, 33 and 34.

Crämer is 16in (41cm) tall.

Pattern layout for Crämer

▦ Indicates pattern to be placed with printed side down.

First... You can reproduce Crämer's unique peach-colored fur by following the instructions on page 36 titled **Dyeing**. ***This must be done before any other steps can be taken.***

Step One:

1. Mount pattern onto sturdy material *i.e.* cardboard and cut out.
2. Trace pattern onto fabric backing using permanent marker and following layout shown on this page. Make sure arrows go in the same direction as nap.
3. Transfer all markings.
4. Cut out taking care to cut fabric backing and not fur on the other side.

Step Two: Sewing (pages 38-39)
Step Three: Head, Eyes and Ears (pages 40-41)
Step Four: Nose and Mouth (page 44)
Step Five: Assembly (pages 46-47)
Step Six: Finishing (pages 48-49)

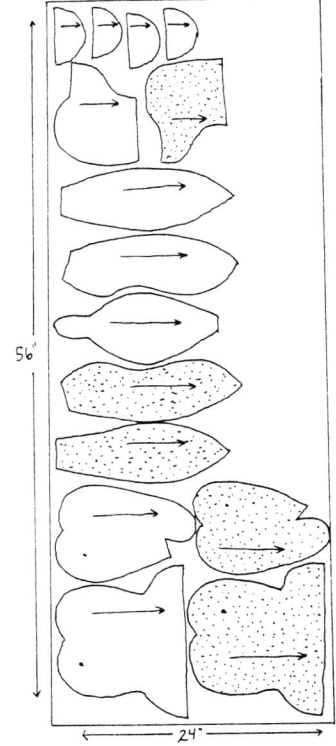

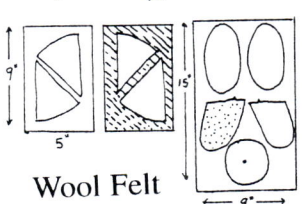

Wool Felt

MUSICAL JOPI
Circa 1930. 15in (38cm).

MUSICAL JOPI

Materials

You will need a piece of mohair or synthetic plush 56in (142cm) wide by 18in (46cm) long. The fur should be 3/4in (2cm) in length.
Tools. Please refer to page 35.

10in (25cm) by 9in (23cm) wool felt for pads
4 1-3/4in (5cm) fiberboard disks for arms
4 1-1/2in (4cm) fiberboard disks for legs
2 2-1/2in (6cm) fiberboard disks for neck
10 metal washers
5 metal cotter pins
2 14mm amber glass eyes
Polyester fiberfill for stuffing
Black pearl cotton for nose, mouth and claws
Button/Carpet thread for closing seams and affixing ears and eyes
Basic Hints. Please refer to pages 32, 33 and 34.

Jopi is 15in (38cm) tall.

Pattern layout for Jopi

Indicates pattern to be placed with printed side down.

First... You can reproduce Jopi's green-tipped fur by following the instructions on page 37 titled **Dyeing**. ***This must be done before any other steps can be taken.***

Step One:

1. Mount pattern onto sturdy material i.e. cardboard and cut out.
2. Trace pattern onto fabric backing using permanent marker and following layout shown on this page. Make sure arrows go in the same direction as nap.
3. Transfer all markings.
4. Cut out taking care to cut fabric backing and not fur on the other side.

Step Two: Sewing (pages 38-39)
Step Three: Head, Eyes and Ears (pages 40-41)
Step Four: Nose and Mouth (page 44)
Step Five: Assembly (pages 46-47)
Step Six: Finishing (pages 48-49)

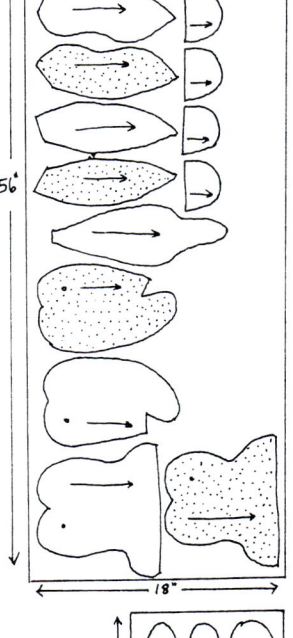

CHURCHILL
Unidentified British manufacturer. Circa 1930.
18in (46cm).

CHURCHILL

Materials

You will need a piece of mohair or synthetic plush 56in (142cm) wide by 22in (56cm) long. The fur should be 1/2in (1cm) in length.
Tools. Please refer to page 35.

18in (46cm) by 5in (13cm) wool felt for pads
4 1-3/4in (5cm) fiberboard disks for arms
4 2-1/2in (6cm) fiberboard disks for legs
2 2-1/2in (6cm) fiberboard disks for neck
10 metal washers
5 metal cotter pins
2 14mm clear glass eyes
Polyester fiberfill for stuffing
Black pearl cotton for nose, mouth and claws
Button/Carpet thread for closing seams and affixing eyes and ears
1 yard 1-1/2in (4cm) wide purple satin ribbon
Basic Hints. Please refer to pages 32, 33 and 34.

***Churchill** is 18in (46cm) tall.*

Pattern layout for Churchill

Indicates pattern to be placed with printed side down.

First... You can reproduce Churchill's lavender fur by following the instructions on page 36 titled **Dyeing. *This must be done before any other steps can be taken.***

Step One:

1. Mount pattern onto sturdy material *i.e. cardboard and cut out.*
2. Trace pattern onto fabric backing using permanent marker and following layout shown on this page. Make sure arrows go in the same direction as nap.
3. Transfer all markings.
4. Cut out taking care to cut fabric backing and not fur on the other side.

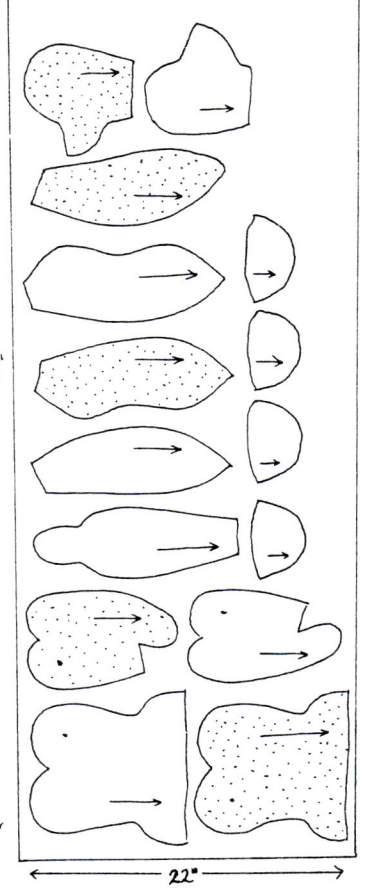

Step Two: Sewing (pages 38-39)
Step Three: Head, Eyes and Ears (pages 40-41)
Step Four: Nose and Mouth (page 45)
Step Five: Assembly (pages 46-47)
Step Six: Finishing (pages 48-49)

CHAD
Chad Valley. Circa 1940.
13in (33cm).

CHAD

Materials

You will need a piece of mohair or synthetic plush 56in (142cm) wide by 12in (31cm) long. The fur should be 1/2in (1cm) in length.
Tools. Please refer to page 35.

14in (36cm) by 4in (10cm) wool felt for pads
4in (10cm) by 5in (13cm) stiff cardboard
4 1-3/4in (5cm) fiberboard disks for arms
4 1-3/4in. (5cm) fiberboard disks for legs
2 2in (5cm) fiberboard disks for neck
10 metal washers
5 metal cotter pins
2 9mm amber eyes
Polyester fiberfill for stuffing
Black pearl cotton for nose, mouth and claws
Button/Carpet thread for closing seams and affixing ears and eyes
Basic Hints. Please refer to pages 32, 33 and 34.

First... You can reproduce Chad's mauve fur by following the instructions on page 36 titled **Dyeing.** *This must be done before any other steps can be taken.*

Step One:

1. Mount pattern onto sturdy material *i.e. cardboard and cut out.*
2. Trace pattern onto fabric backing using permanent marker and following layout shown on this page. Make sure arrows go in the same direction as nap.
3. Transfer all markings.
4. Cut out taking care to cut fabric backing and not fur on the other side.

Step Two: Sewing (pages 38-39)
Step Three: Head, Eyes and Ears
(pages 40-41)
Step Four: Nose and Mouth (page 45)
Step Five: Assembly (pages 46-47)
Step Six: Finishing (pages 48-49)

Chad is 13in (33cm) tall.
Pattern layout for Chad

Indicates pattern to be placed with printed side down.

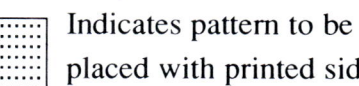
Wool Felt

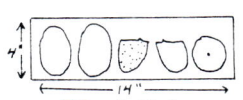
Cardboard

Basic Hints

*BEFORE YOU START, ALWAYS READ THE ENTIRE PATTERN!

NAP OF THE FUR: The nap of the fur is determined by stroking the fur. If it lays down smoothly, that is the direction of the nap. When the fur ruffles, or stands up when stroked, that is against the nap.

LAYING OUT THE PATTERN: Always lay out a pattern on the back of the fabric. Mark direction of nap with a little arrow and take your time! Arrows on pattern shapes should correspond with arrows on fabric. Check that you have reversed pieces where needed; use indelible felt pen to mark and don't forget to mark the joint holes along the way.

CUTTING OUT: Cutting on a flat surface, use a small pair of sharp, pointed scissors. Be careful to cut the backing only, not the fur. Take your time!

Due to the expense of mohair, the illustrated examples of the pattern layout for each bear is the most economical way to avoid wasting material. The pattern pieces from the book can be photocopied or traced.

Make sure the pieces of fabric are cut on the straight of the grain. This prevents twisting and stretching problems when stuffing.

When cutting around the traced lines of the pattern pieces on the fabric backing, take particular care to cut exactly on the line and not outside. Even a slight change to the pattern will alter the look of the bear (especially his face). You could even end up with one limb larger than the other.

PINNING: Pieces are all sewn inside out. To keep flat use plenty of pins with heads pointing to the outside.

STITCHING: Make sure your stitch tension and seam allowances are the same throughout making the entire bear. In hand stitching, if the needle does not go through the fabric, rub the needle on wax candle.

STUFFING: Stuff firmly, especially the head. When stuffing head, use thumbs to indent where eye sockets will be.

EYES: Important safety note: Eyes used on original bears were shoe-button or glass. However, if the bear is made for a child's toy, substitute plastic safety eyes.

FINISHING TOUCH: Use a stiff brush or fine wire brush to pull fur caught in seams.

Basic Hints

*BEFORE YOU START, ALWAYS READ THE ENTIRE PATTERN!

RECREATING TIPS: To achieve the closest possible resemblance to the original antique bear, you must not only follow the directions closely, but also study the photograph of the original antique. Take into consideration certain looks only come with generations of love.

Studying body characteristics attributed to various manufacturers and/or countries will also aid in recreating authentic looking antique bears.

With Mitchom, you'll see that his right arm shows great loss of fur. Apparently, the bear's original young owner favored the right arm of his companion when carrying him around with him.

The loved look of Roosevelt and Liberty is the result of the excelsior in the body breaking down. This creates the appealing, old, slouched look. You can get this look in your rendition by understuffing the body. (Please see directions for Roosevelt and Liberty).

Another appealing trait of early bears is the worn fur around the snout. This probably can be attributed to all the hundreds of kisses the bear received from his young friends. You too can easily duplicate this look by trimming the fur around the snout after the head is completed (please see directions for each bear for details).

Facial expressions are, of course, one of the most important features of any bear. In addition to the pattern designed to represent the original, the stuffing of the face and placement of the eyes all contribute to that precious look of a perfect rendition.

Unfortunately, the concertina, squeeze-box type music box originally concealed in the body of our Jopi bear and in the head of Crämer the Clown, is no longer available today. However, there are key-wind music boxes available that produce beautiful sounds with numerous melodies. The musical mechanism is concealed in a plastic box. If you wish to enclose the music box in your Jopi or Crämer recreation, insert the music box prior to closing the back seam on the bear's torso. Make sure the stuffing completely conceals and pads the box, leaving the key protruding from the back center seam for turning. Sew the back body seam neatly and firmly (using a ladder stitch), around the key

Basic Hints

*BEFORE YOU START, ALWAYS READ THE ENTIRE PATTERN!

CREATING BEAR DESIGNS OF YOUR OWN: You may also use these patterns to create your very own bear designs. There are a number of methods to follow to achieve these results.

The simplest method is to reduce or enlarge the pattern on a photocopy machine. Maybe you would like your bear to have a slightly larger body or longer arms or legs, bigger ears or longer snout. You'll be amazed how much fun you'll have and the satisfaction of creating wonderful bears with just a few small changes. Remember to note the percentage you increased or decreased your pattern for your records.

Different fabrics or mohair changes the look of a bear tremendously. Even the length of the fur can make a dramatic difference to the overall look of the bear. However, it is not a good idea to use fur any longer than 1/4in (.5cm) on 3in (7cm) to 6in (15cm) bears, as their features may seem to small.

Another change which greatly alters the facial appearance is the size, type and placement of the eyes. Large eyes give the bear a youthful, soft look. Small eyes placed close together create a quizzical and rather amused look.

The detailed diagrams of noses and mouths give you many options. Switch nose and mouth designs on the bears. Varying the colors of thread for the nose and mouth is yet another simple way of creating your very own bear. Change the size and location of nose and/or mouth.

Originally, teddy bears paw pads were made of quality thick beige felt. However, leather and suede work well and have a nice feel. You may try reversing the mohair which gives an entirely different look to the paw pads. Another fun idea is coordinating and contrasting printed fabrics for a completely individual appearance.

Tools and Fabrics

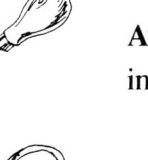 **Long Needle:** To sew up seam openings; to sew on ears and eyes; to sew on nose, mouth and claws.

 **Needle Nose Pliers:** To turn and tighten cotter pins.

Awl: To poke holes in fabric for joints.

 **Brush:** To brush out fur from seams.

 **Scissors:** To snip and cut!

Wooden Dowel: To stuff bear limbs firmly.

Most of the high-quality antique bears, including those of my collection represented here, were made of mohair, which comes from Angora goats. However, less expensive acrylics may be used and your bear will still be appealing and look about the same. Take into consideration that some acrylic fabrics stretch more than mohair. An overall rule-of-thumb is that the smaller the bear, the shorter the length of the fur should be.

Mohair can be straight, wavy, stringy, distressed (a process similar to giving hair a perm) and dense. Whether German, American or English, long or short, it comes in a variety of colors and can be spun to an extremely fine count. The thinner the individual strands, the softer they feel.

As some of the colors of the fabric for antique bears (for bears fabric color, refer to illustrations) may not be available, you may wish to dye your fabric. Always follow the package instructions! Just remember, it is almost impossible to lighten a dark fabric, but easy to darken a light one. Acrylic fabrics will not take dye as well as mohair.

DYEING

CRÄMER, CHURCHILL AND CHAD:

Important: Use white mohair for best results

Materials
Large container (sink or dish)
3 gallons of boiling water
Liquid dye
Cramer: One half cap-full of Red
           Two cap-fulls of True Yellow
Chad: Three cap-fulls of Mauve
Churchill: Three cap-fulls of Purple
(These amounts vary depending upon the type of fur used.)
Small fabric swatch sample
Rinse bath:
    2 gallons cool water
    1/2 cup vinegar
    1/2 cup salt
Wooden spoon

1. Fill the large container with the boiling water.
2. Add recommended amount of dye and stir.
3. Wet sample swatch.
4. Dip into dye bath and note time it takes for sample to reach desired color.
5. Then, allow the color to get one shade darker because it will dry a shade lighter.
6. Now, wet entire piece of fabric and dip into dye bath.
7. Stir constantly with a wooden spoon to get even color.
8. Remove from dye bath and soak in Rinse bath.
9. Wring out and allow to air dry. Do not use dryer.

DYEING

Musical JOPI (just the tips of his fur is dyed)
Important: Use off-white mohair for best results.

Materials
Large container
One cup of boiling water
One capful of Green liquid dye
Smaller container
Small piece of natural sponge
Larger natural sponge
Rubber gloves
Rinse Bath:
    1 cup cool water
    1/4 cup vinegar
    1/4 cup salt

Note: Do not wet fur before dyeing.
1. In a small container, mix boiling water and dye.
2. Dip small piece of sponge into the dye and wring it as dry as possible.
3. Using the larger sponge to keep fabric backing and base of fur dry, blot tips of fur with dye.
4. Dip small sponge in Rinse Bath and wring dry.
5. Using the larger sponge to keep fabric backing and base of fur dry, blot tips of fur with sponge.
6. Allow to air dry.

Step Two: SEWING

**Pin all pieces before Sewing
Use 1/4in (.65cm) seam allowances.
Sew all pieces with right sides together.**

1. Sew 'head sides' together.

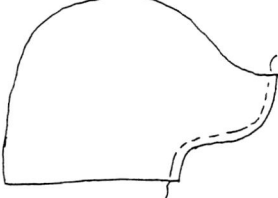

2. Set in 'head gussett' between 'head sides' and sew starting at nose.

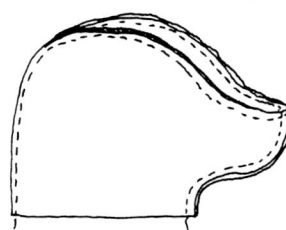

3. Sew 'body back' pieces together leaving opening at back.

4. Sew 'body front' pieces together.

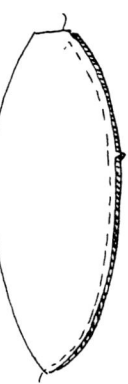

5. Sew 'body front' and 'body back' together at side seams.

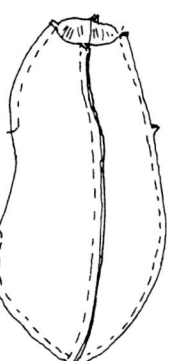

6. Sew pad onto arm matching notches.

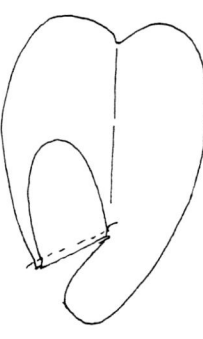

Turn all pieces right-side out.

Step Two: SEWING

Pin all pieces before Sewing
Use 1/4in (.65cm) seam allowances.
Sew all pieces with right sides together.

7. Fold arm in half along line and sew leaving opening at top for stuffing. Repeat with other arm.
   Note: Before turning right side out clip 1/8in (.31cm) at wrist as indicated on arm pattern (through felt and fabric).

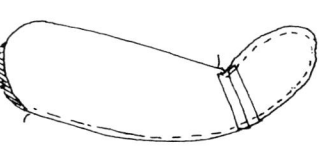

8. Fold leg in half and sew together leaving top open for stuffing. Repeat with other leg.

9. Snip 1/8in (.31cm) back of heel.

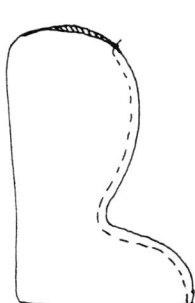
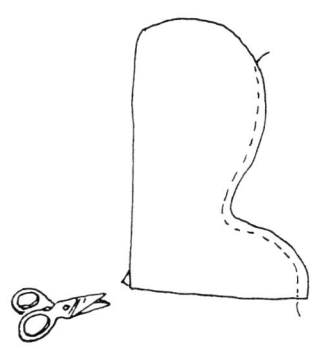

10. Set in felt foot pad and sew from the toe to the heel on one side of the foot and from the toe to the heel on the other. Repeat with other leg.

11. Sew ears together.

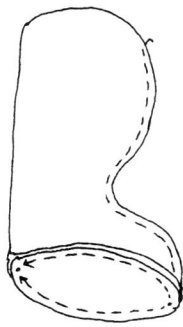

Turn all pieces right-side out.

Step Three: HEAD, EYES, AND EARS

HEAD

1. Use running stitch around head opening 1/4in (.65cm) from bottom.

    Stuff head firmly - especially the nose.

2. Construct joint using fiberboard disc, metal washer and cotter pin.

3. Place constructed joint in head hole.
   Pull up running stitch tightly around cotter pin.

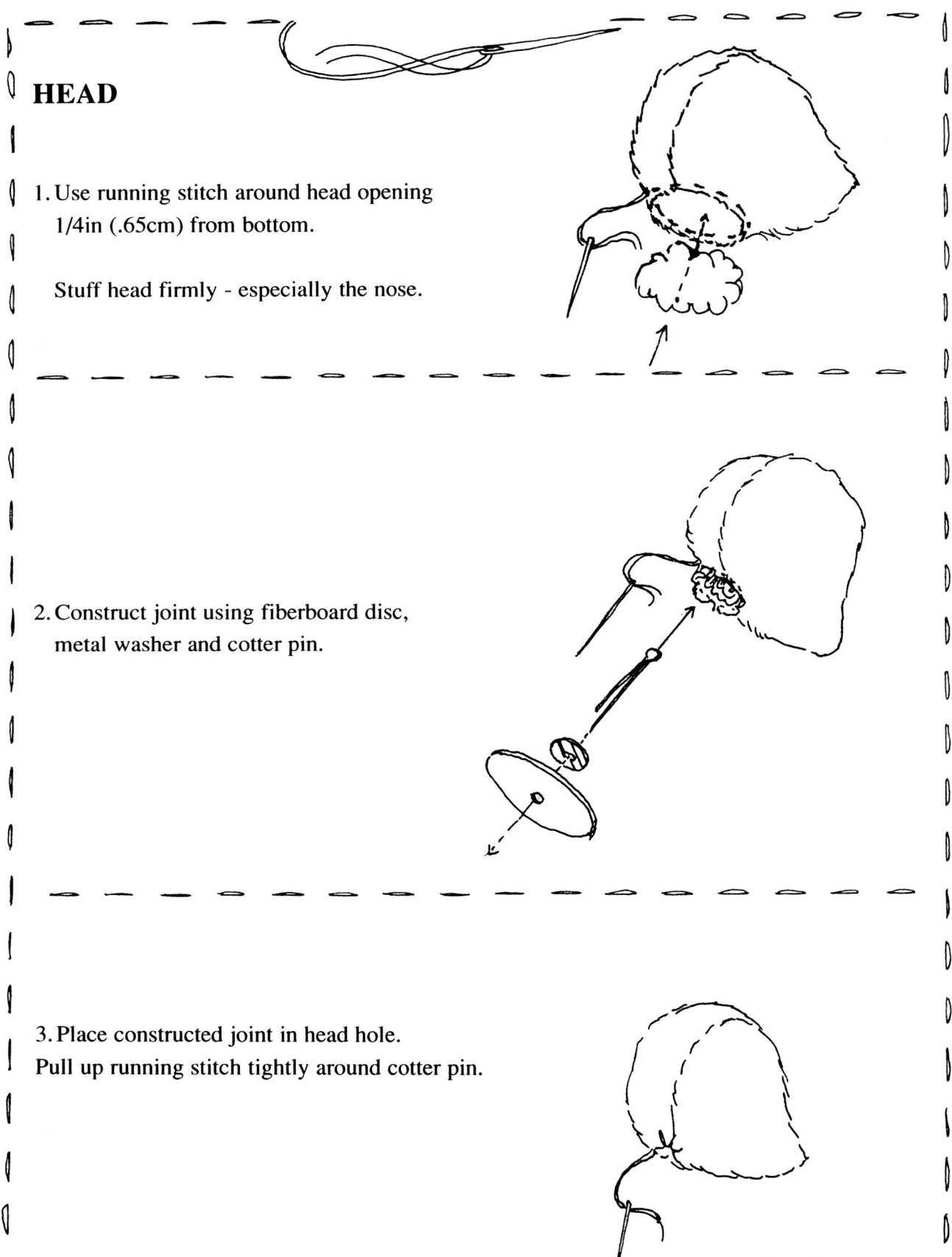

Step Three: HEAD, EYES, AND EARS

EYES

4. Poke holes for eyes using an awl.

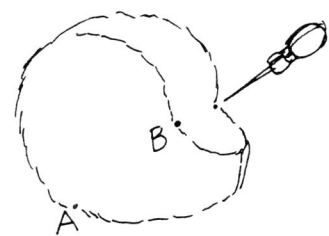

5. Use a long needle with Button/Carpet thread (doubled) knotted at the end. Insert needle at base of neck at point A. Exit at point B.

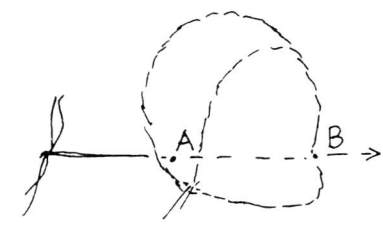

6. Thread shoe button type or glass eye onto needle. Push needle back to point A. Pull tightly, tie ends together and knot. Bury knot in fur.

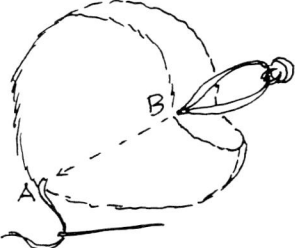

7. Repeat on other side of head with other eye.

   Snip away any fur covering eyes.

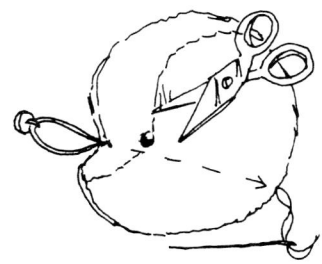

EARS

8. Fold ear opening under 1/4in (.65cm) and close ear opening using a running stitch.

9. Pin ends to head using pattern as guide.

10. Attach to head using Ladder Stitch.

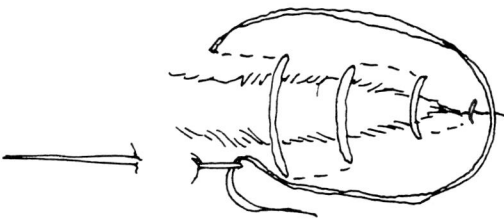

Step Four: NOSE and MOUTH

ROOSEVELT

MITCHOM

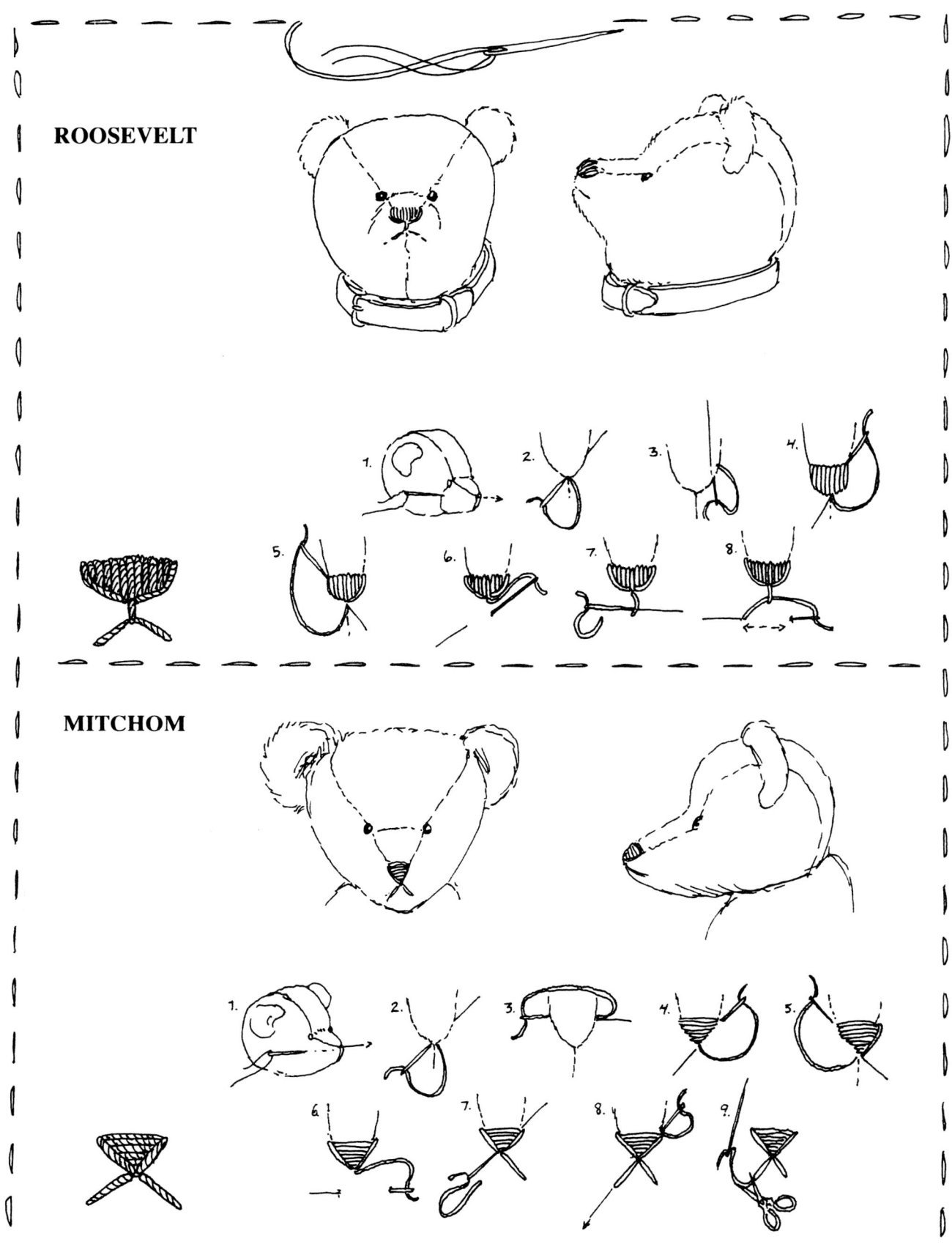

Step Four: NOSE AND MOUTH

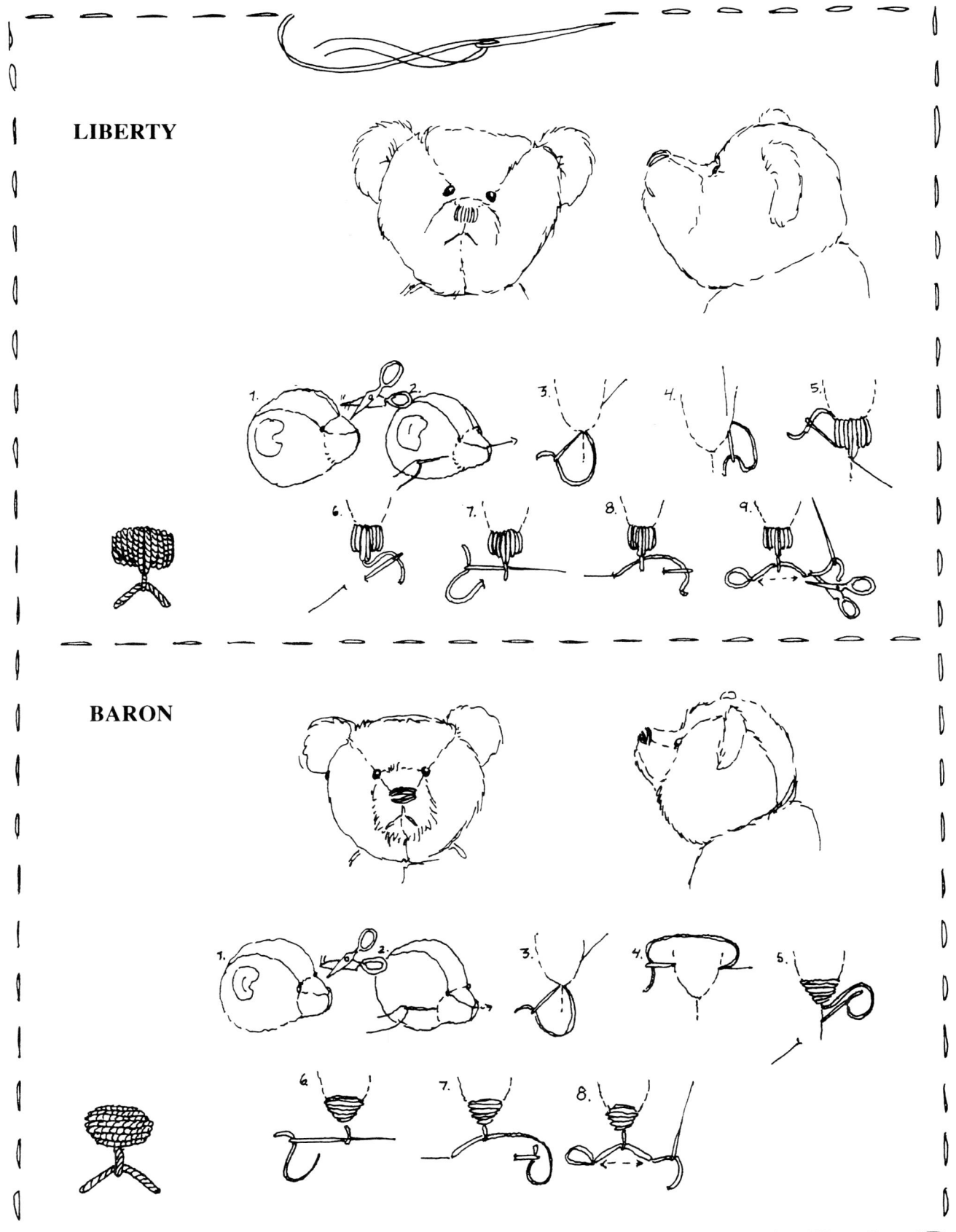

LIBERTY

BARON

Step Four: NOSE AND MOUTH

CRÄMER

JOPI

Step Four: NOSE and MOUTH

CHURCHILL

CHAD

45

Step Five: ASSEMBLY

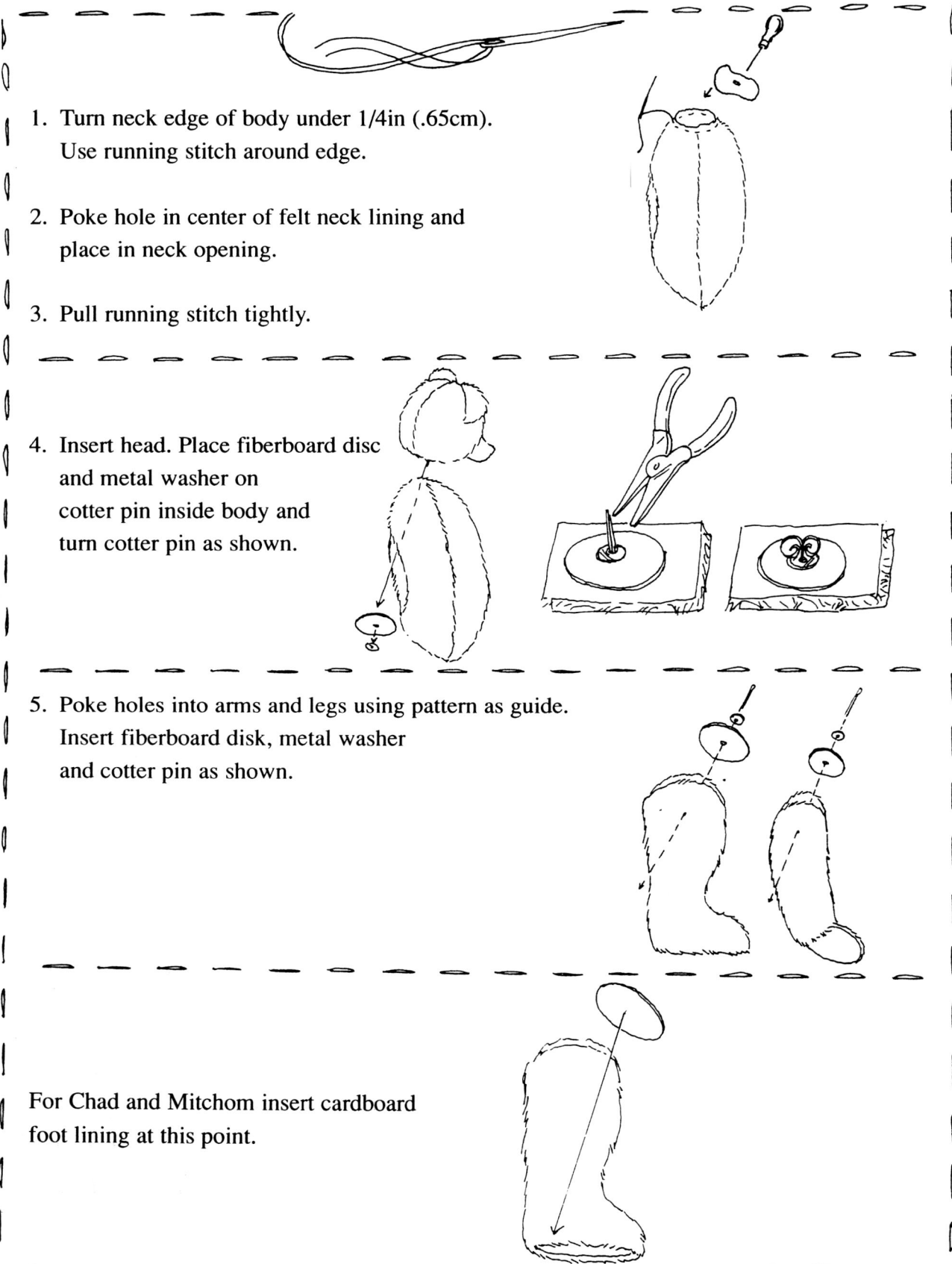

1. Turn neck edge of body under 1/4in (.65cm). Use running stitch around edge.

2. Poke hole in center of felt neck lining and place in neck opening.

3. Pull running stitch tightly.

4. Insert head. Place fiberboard disc and metal washer on cotter pin inside body and turn cotter pin as shown.

5. Poke holes into arms and legs using pattern as guide. Insert fiberboard disk, metal washer and cotter pin as shown.

For Chad and Mitchom insert cardboard foot lining at this point.

Step Five: ASSEMBLY

6. Poke holes into body as shown, insert arms and legs. Place fiberboard disc and metal washer on cotter pin inside body and turn cotter pin.

7. Stuff body and limbs firmly using wooden dowel.

8. Close all seams using ladder stitch.

Step Six: FINISHING TOUCHES

CLAWS:

Follow the arm and leg pattern for each bear to determine the number and the length of their claws.

(All the bears except Churchill and Rolph have claws.)

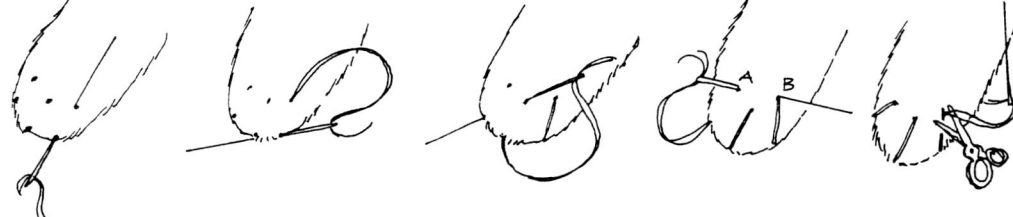

Run needle several times between A and B.

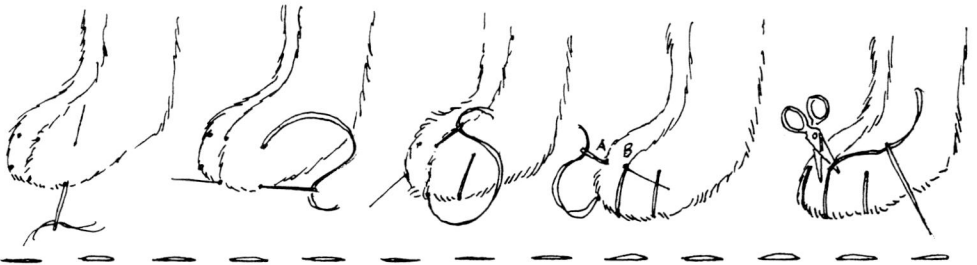

Tie a purple ribbon around Churchill's neck.

...and be sure to brush the fur out of your bear's seams. Isn't he wonderful?

Step Six: FINISHING TOUCHES

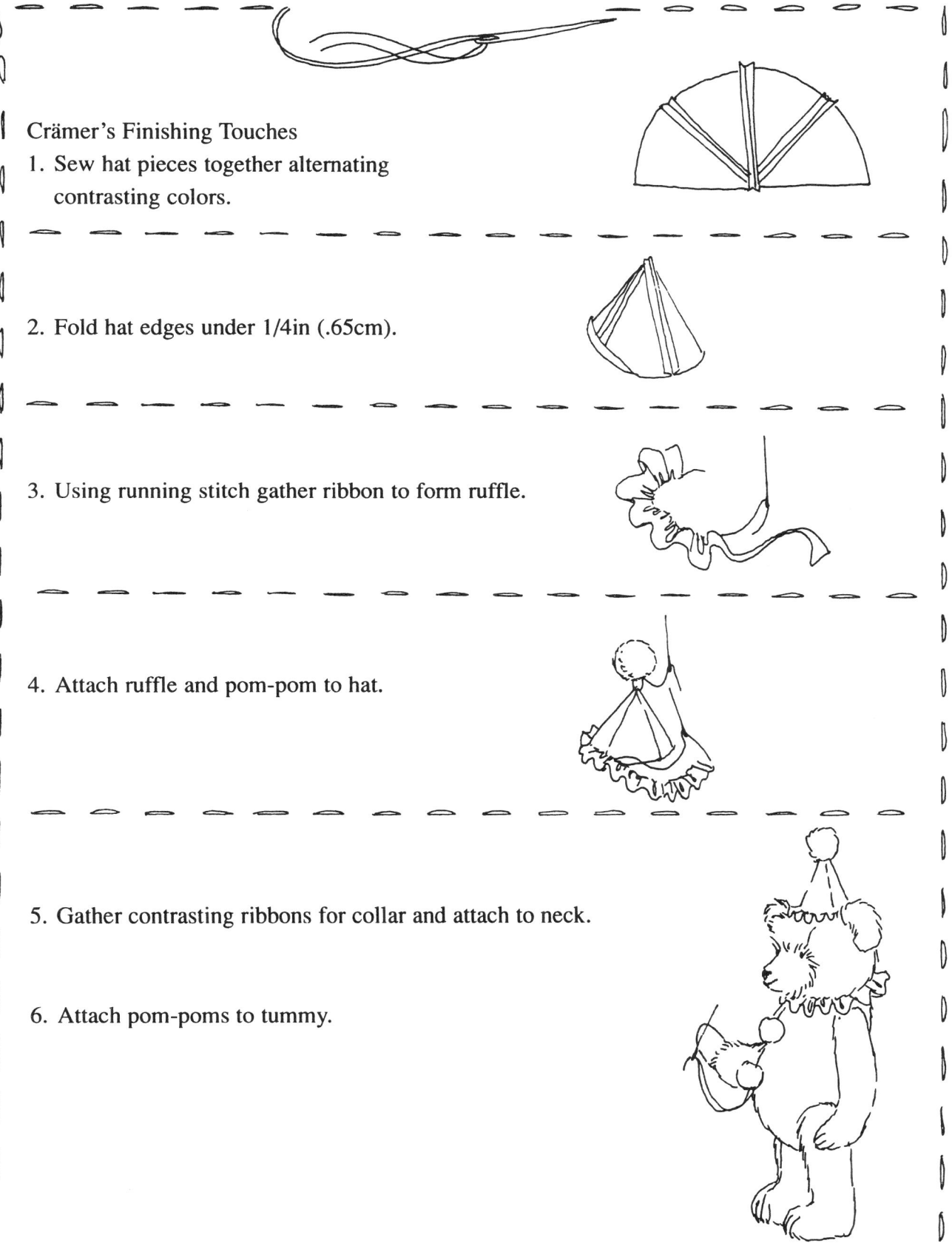

Crämer's Finishing Touches

1. Sew hat pieces together alternating contrasting colors.

2. Fold hat edges under 1/4in (.65cm).

3. Using running stitch gather ribbon to form ruffle.

4. Attach ruffle and pom-pom to hat.

5. Gather contrasting ribbons for collar and attach to neck.

6. Attach pom-poms to tummy.

Step Two: SEWING ROLPH

Machine stitch using 1/4in (.65cm) seams.
Sew all pieces with right sides together.
Refer to the pattern for marks.

1. Sew neck dart on side head by first folding on the solid line, then, sewing on dotted line.

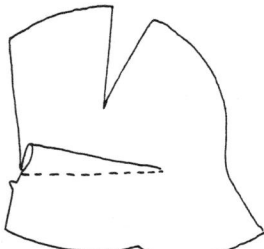

2. Sew ears. Turn right side out.

3. Place ear into open dart at top of side head. Sew into place.

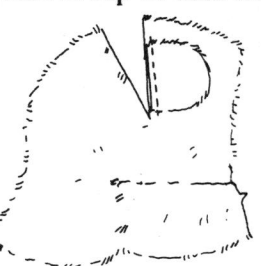

4. Enclose the ear in dart by folding and sewing on dotted line.

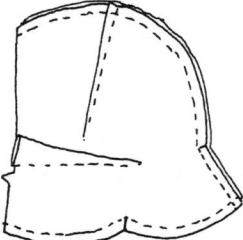

5. Repeat for other side of head. Then, sew both sides of head together. Clip seam allowance where indicated. Turn right side out.

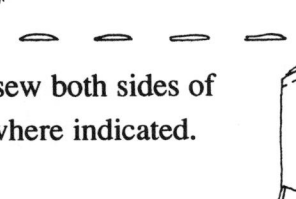

6. Cut along solid line tummy gusset.

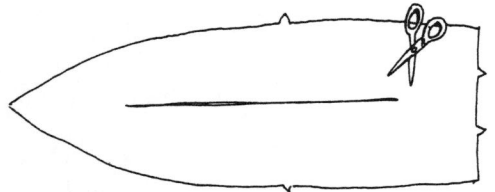

7. Sew along center back seam.

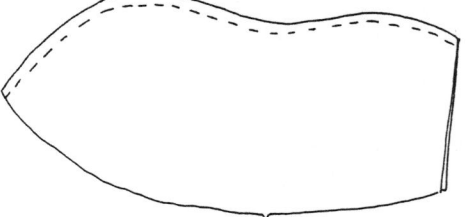

Step Two: SEWING ROLPH

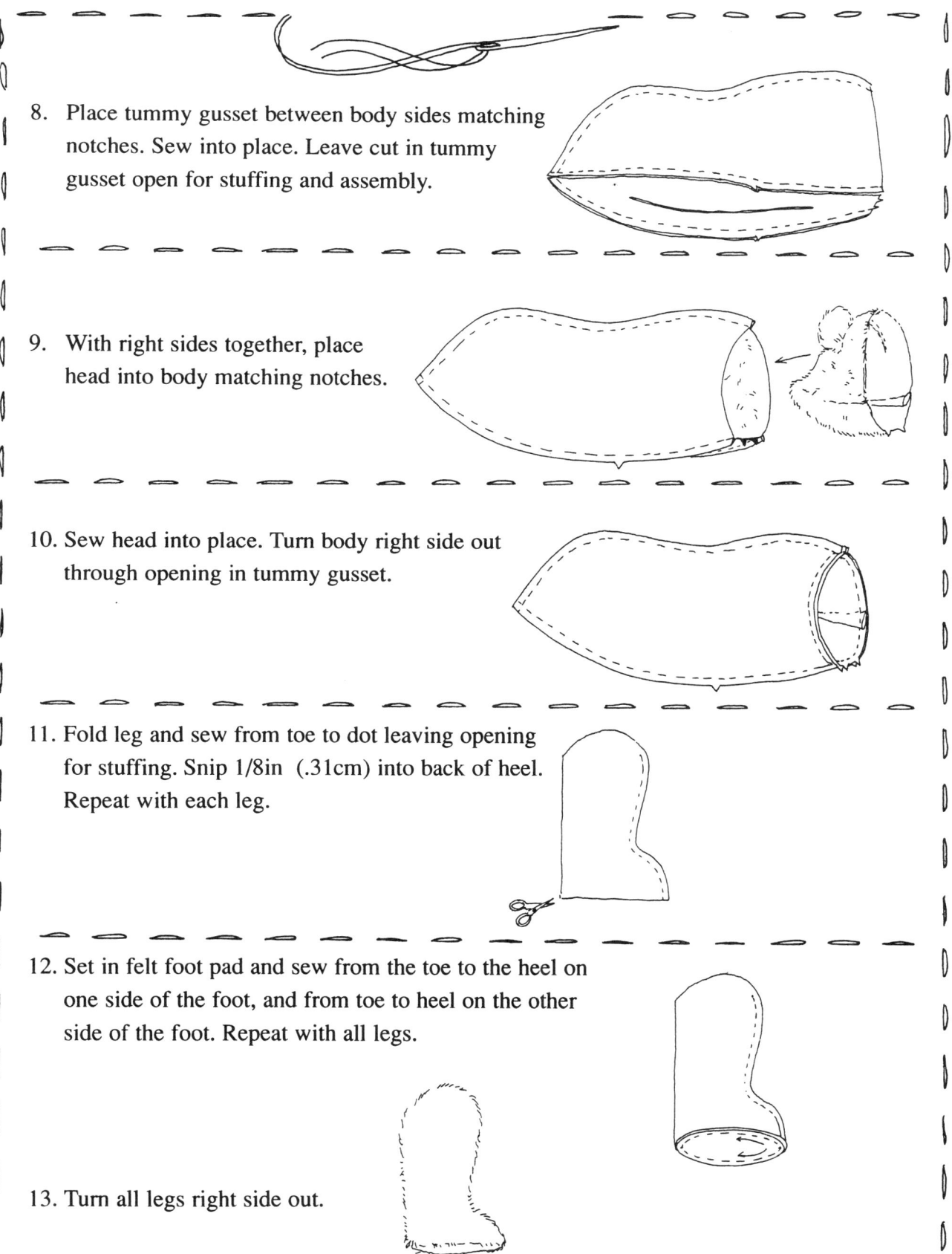

8. Place tummy gusset between body sides matching notches. Sew into place. Leave cut in tummy gusset open for stuffing and assembly.

9. With right sides together, place head into body matching notches.

10. Sew head into place. Turn body right side out through opening in tummy gusset.

11. Fold leg and sew from toe to dot leaving opening for stuffing. Snip 1/8in (.31cm) into back of heel. Repeat with each leg.

12. Set in felt foot pad and sew from the toe to the heel on one side of the foot, and from toe to heel on the other side of the foot. Repeat with all legs.

13. Turn all legs right side out.

Step Three: ASSEMBLING ROLPH

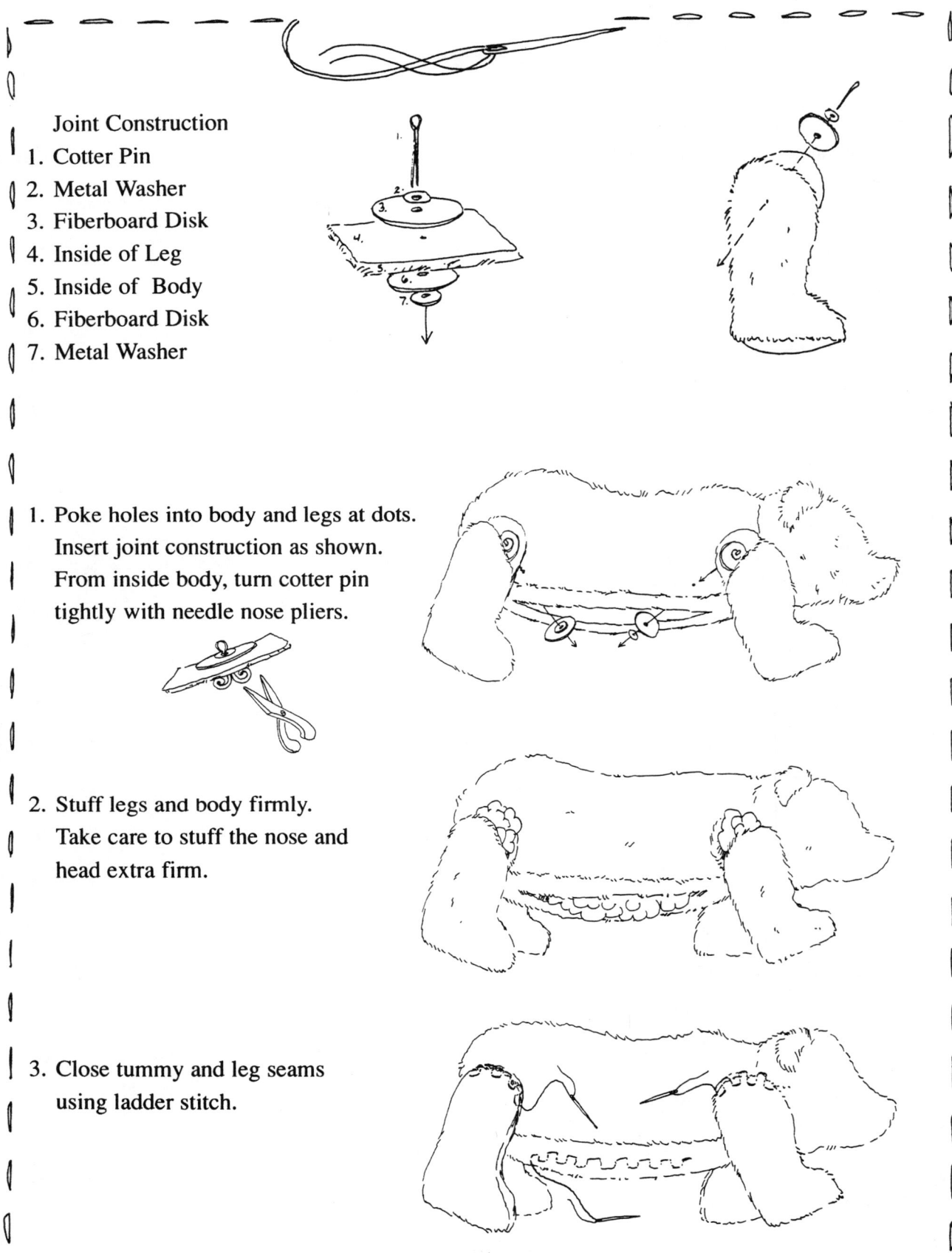

Joint Construction
1. Cotter Pin
2. Metal Washer
3. Fiberboard Disk
4. Inside of Leg
5. Inside of Body
6. Fiberboard Disk
7. Metal Washer

1. Poke holes into body and legs at dots. Insert joint construction as shown. From inside body, turn cotter pin tightly with needle nose pliers.

2. Stuff legs and body firmly. Take care to stuff the nose and head extra firm.

3. Close tummy and leg seams using ladder stitch.

Step Four: ROLPH'S HEADWORK

1. Clip fur from around muzzle and poke holes for eyes using an awl.

2. a. Using Button/Carpet thread (double) knotted at the end, insert needle at base of neck at point A. Exit at point B.
   b. Thread shoe button-type eye onto needle.
   c. Push needle back to point A. Pull tightly, tie ends together and knot. Bury knot in fur.
   d. Repeat on other side of head with other eye.
   e. Snip any fur covering eyes.

3. Apply nose and mouth using the following illustration. To fasten off, insert needle back and forth between C and D twice. Do not pull tight. Snip thread.

53

Step Five: FINISHING ROLPH

...And Don't Forget My Tail!

1. Fold tail in half and sew with right sides together.

2. Turn right side out.

3. Fold under 1/4in (.65cm) and baste using running stitch.

4. Pull up on thread to form curve.

5. Attach to bear's bottom with seam-side down.

THANK YOU!

Patterns

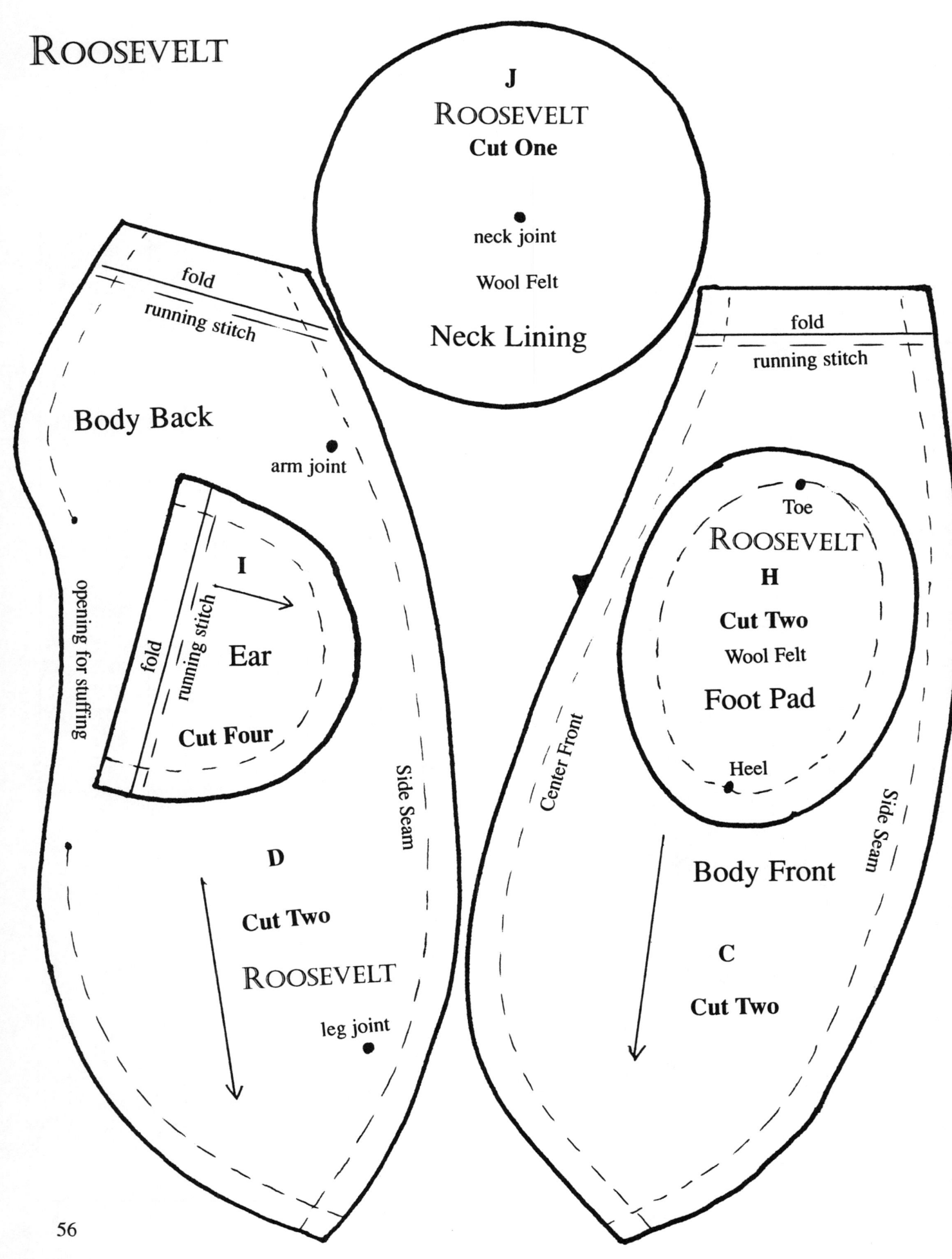

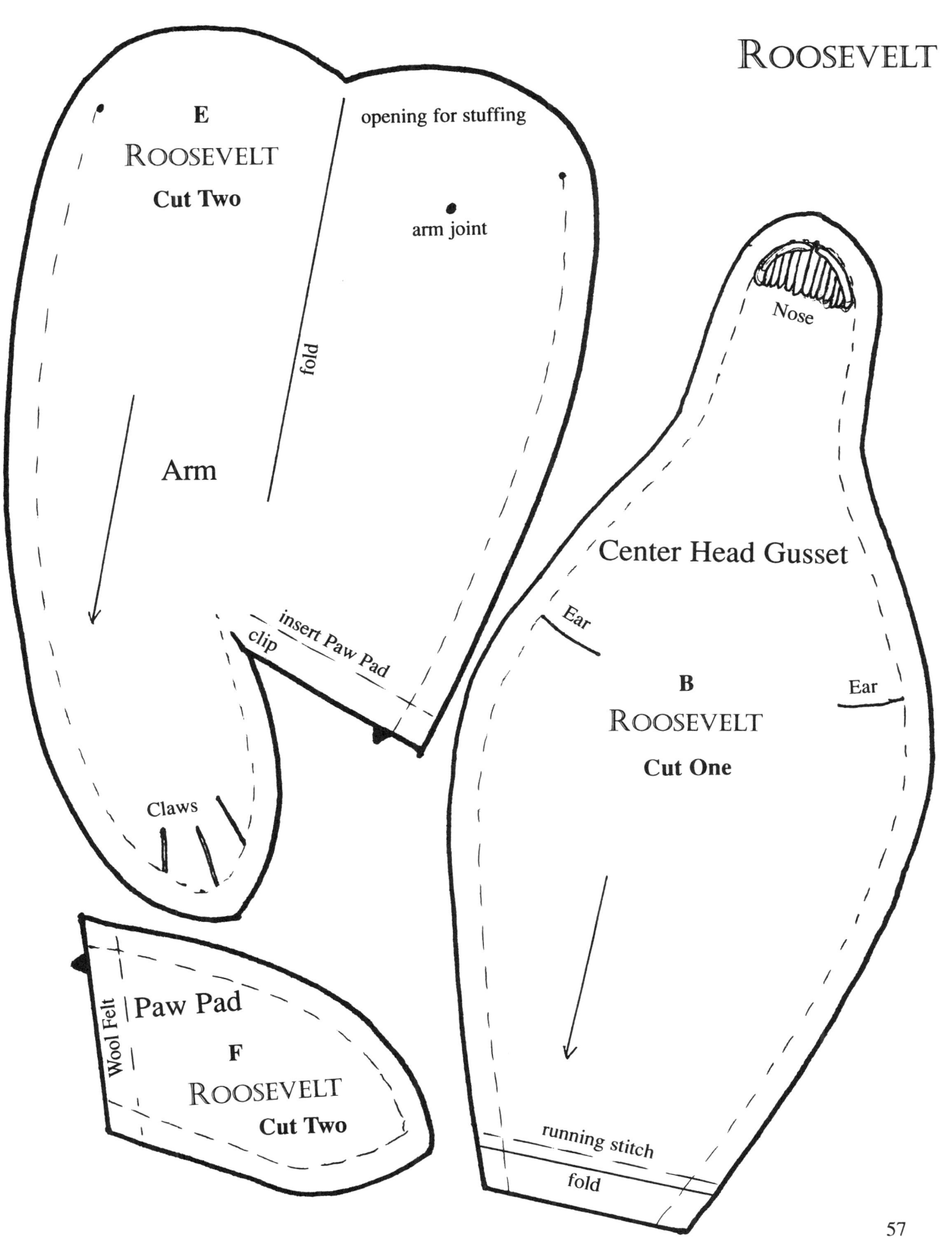

Roosevelt

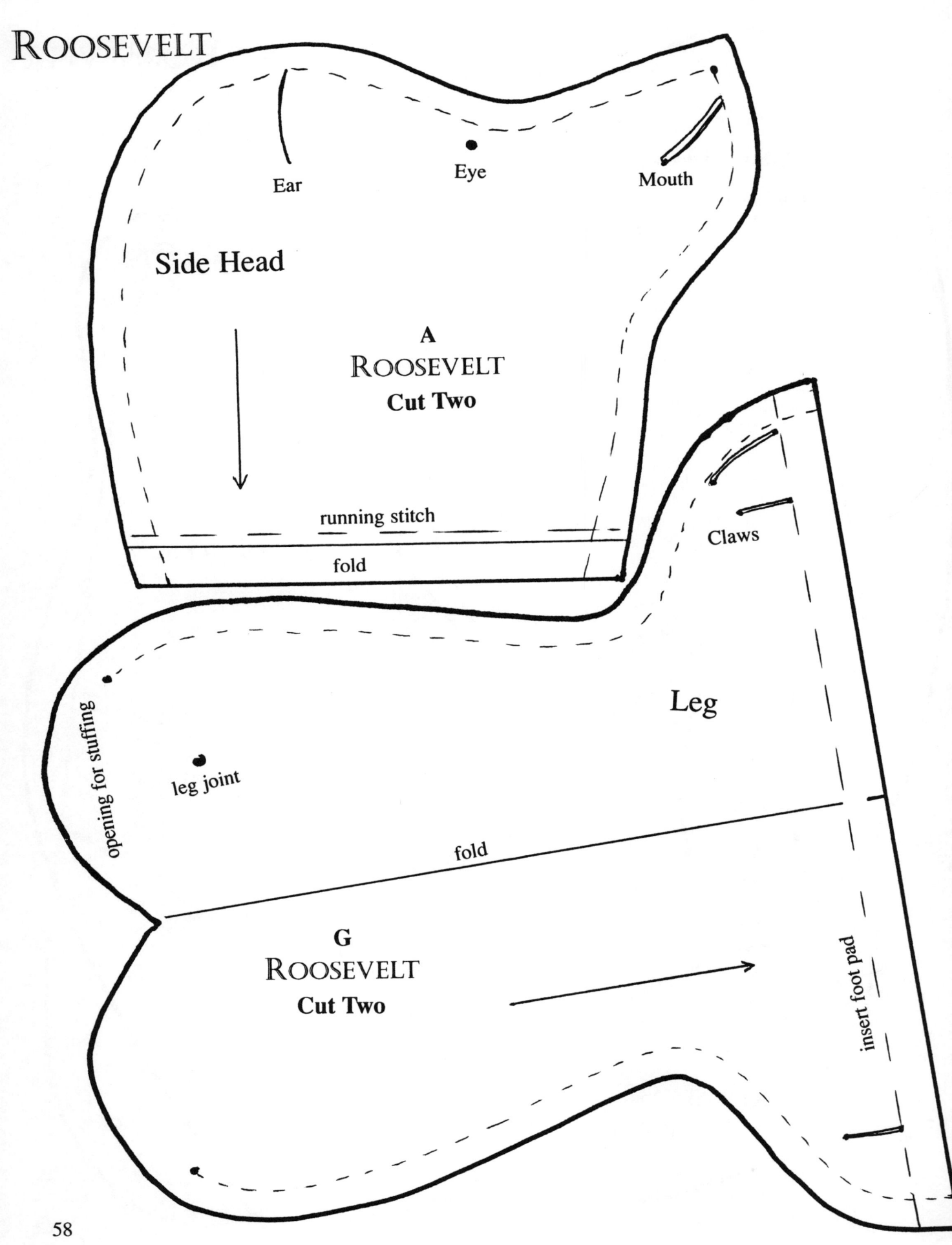

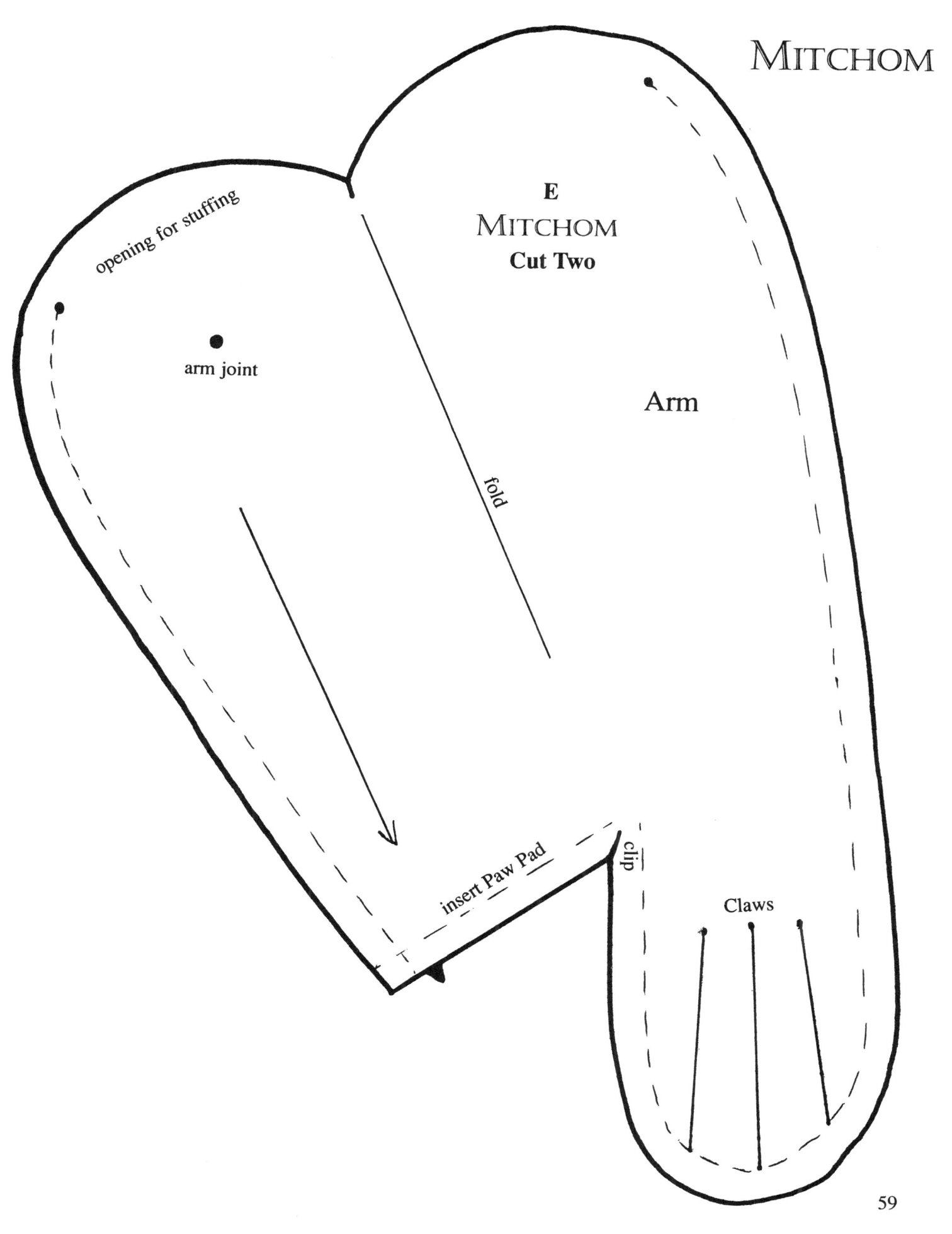

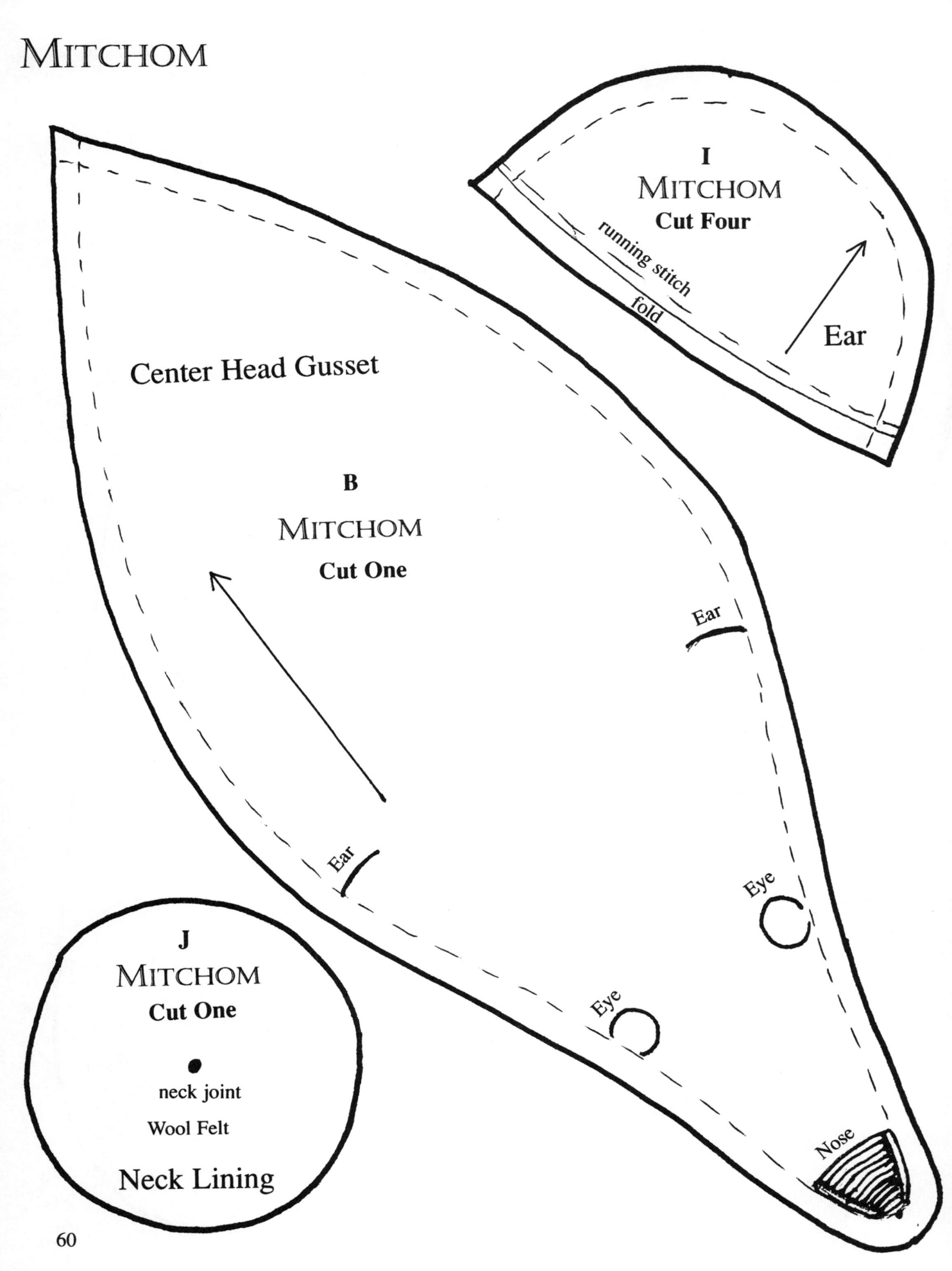

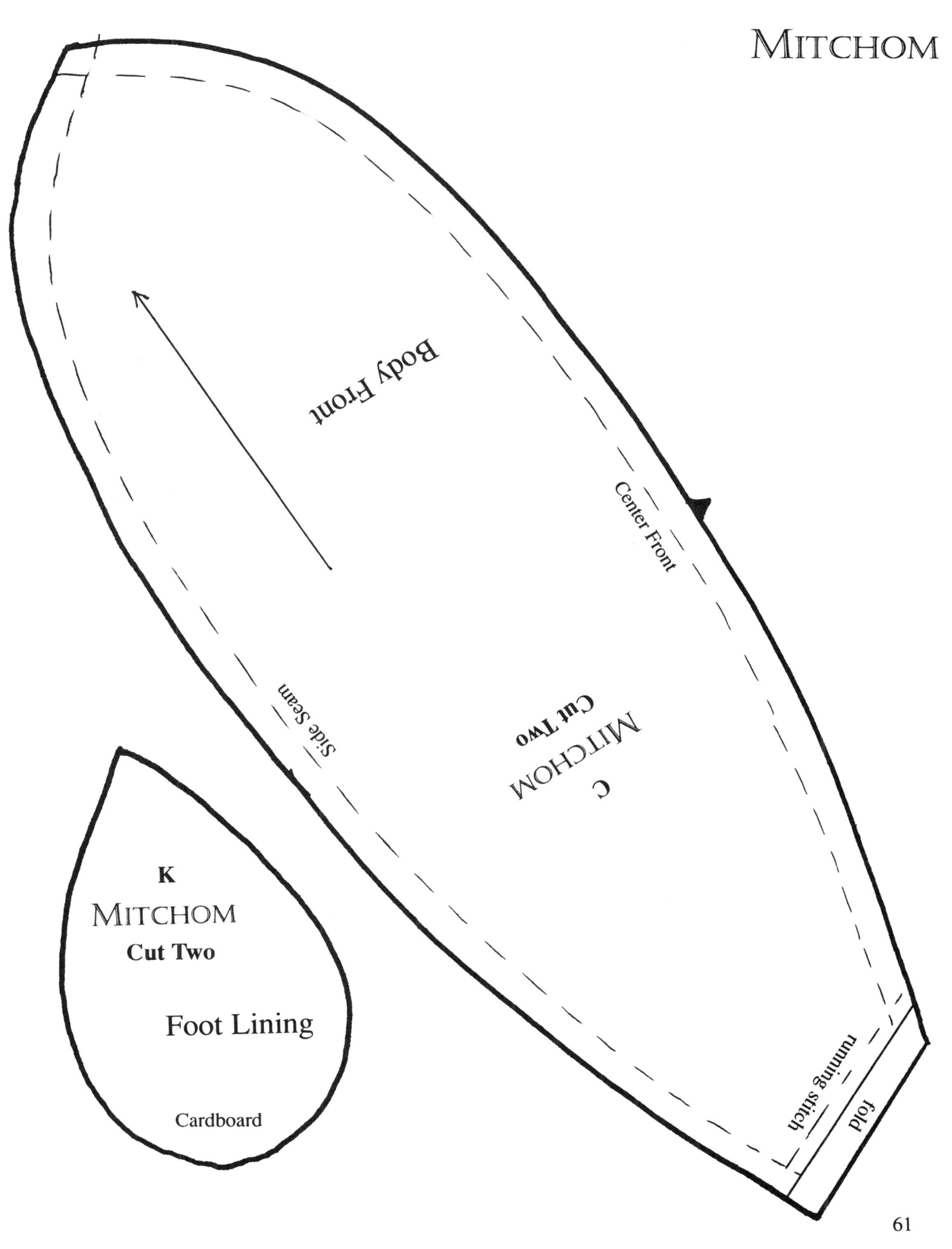

Mitchom

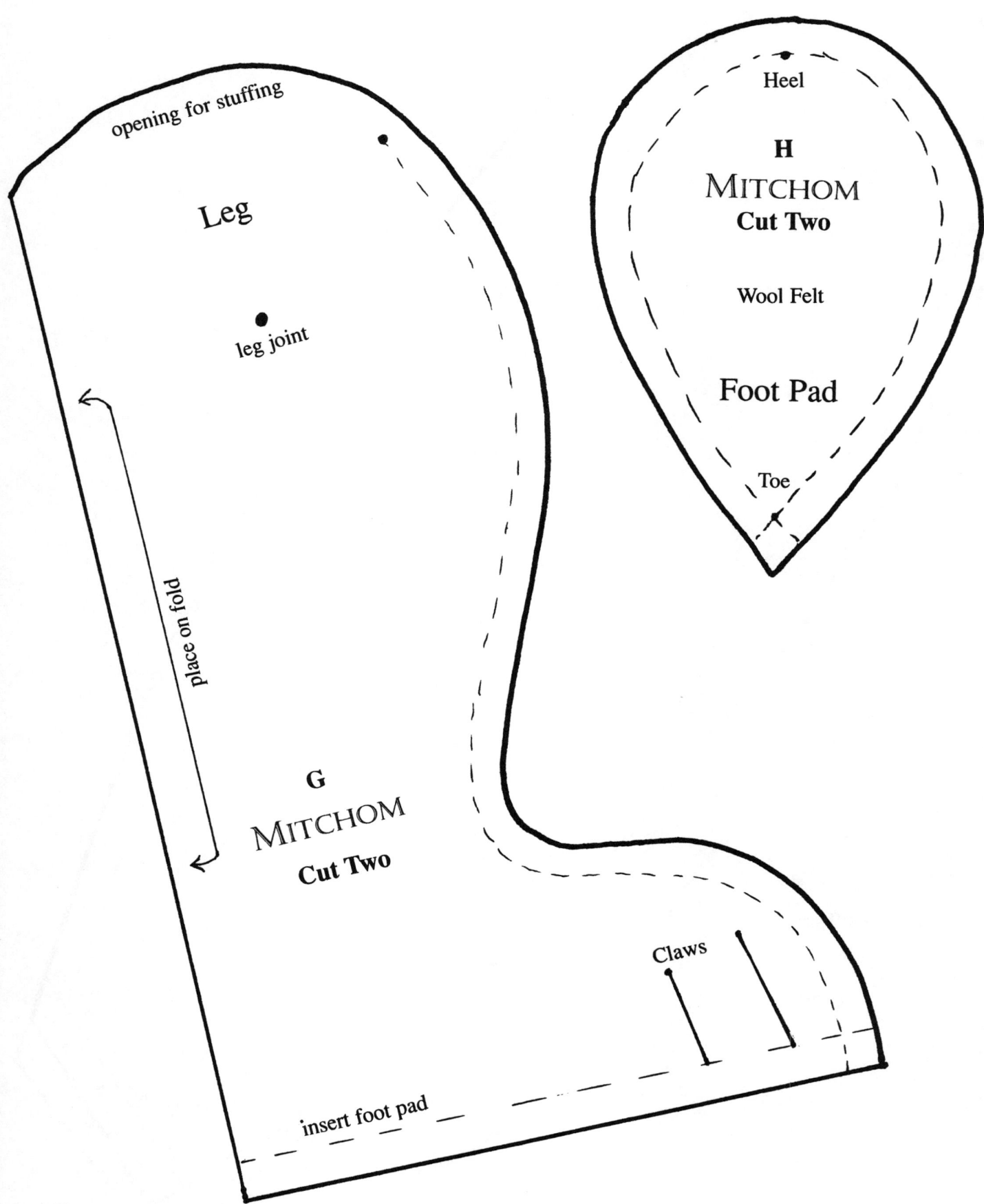

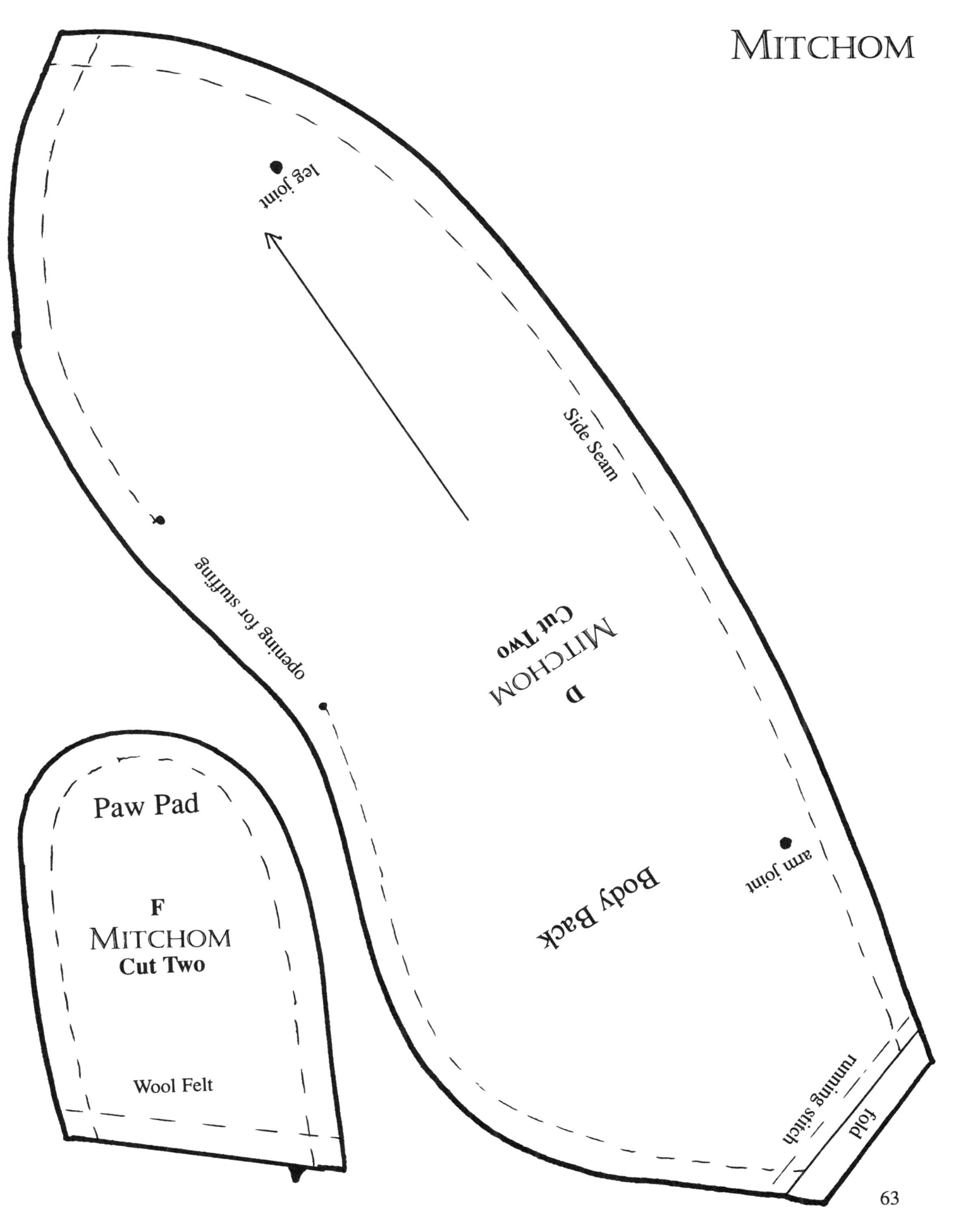

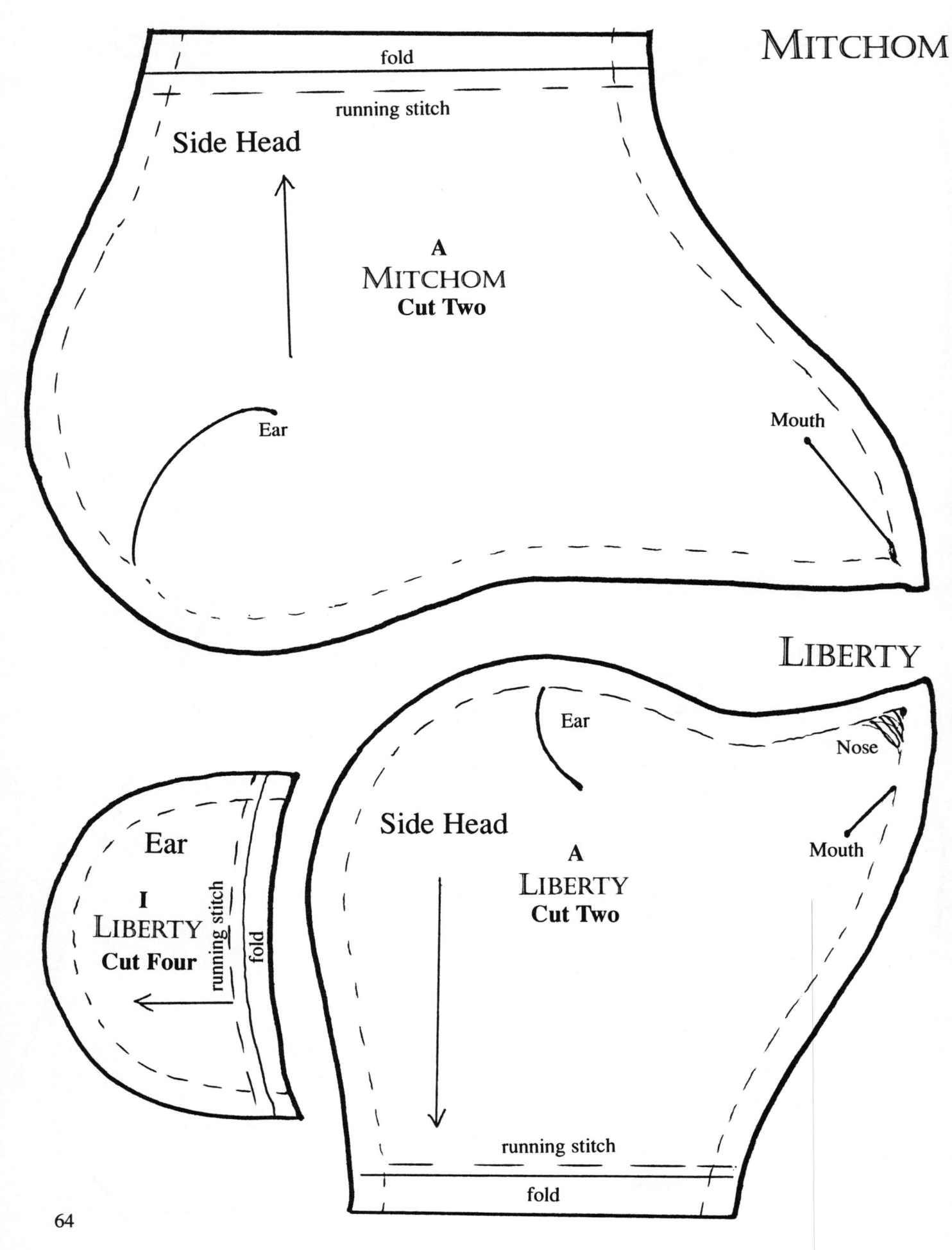

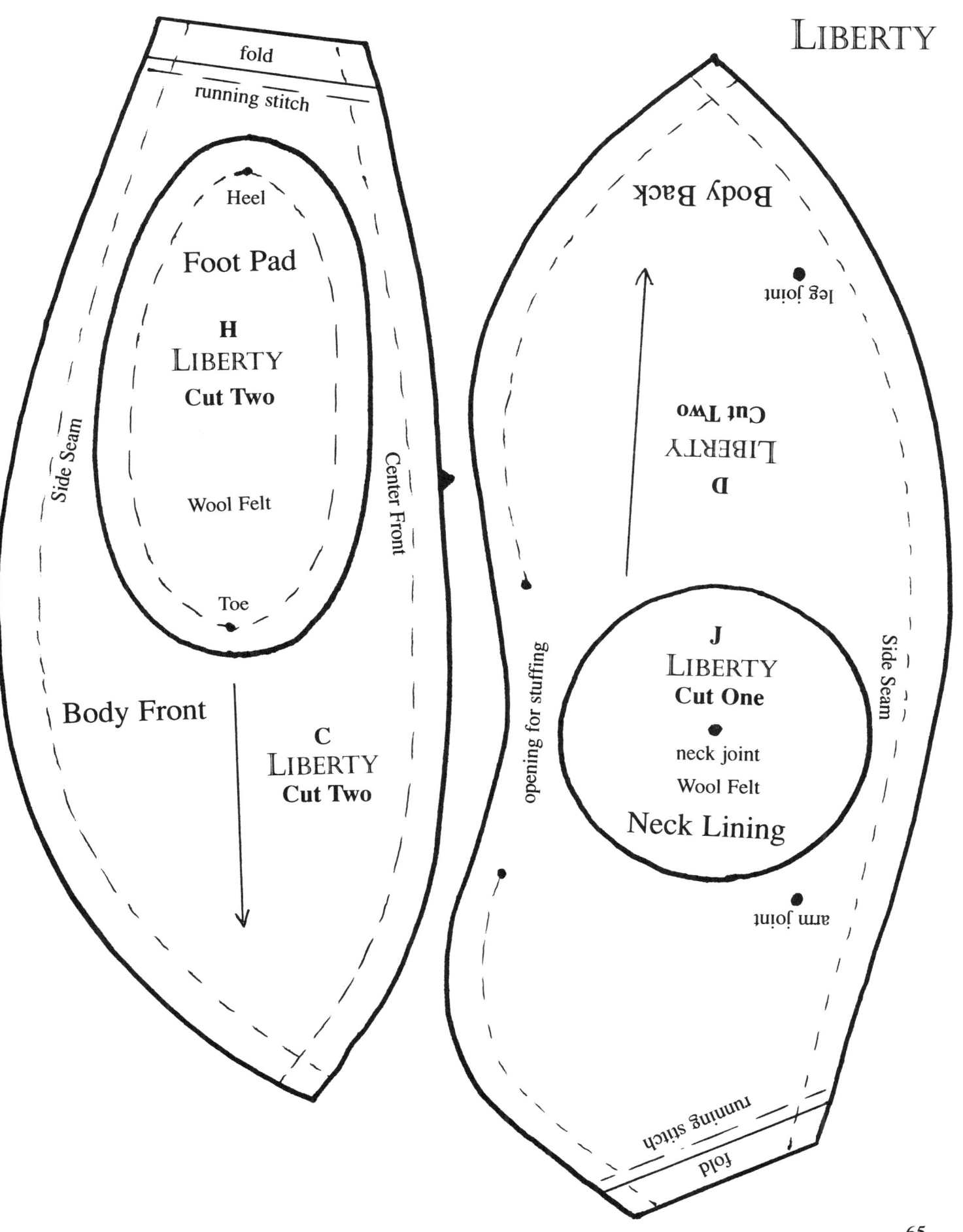

Liberty

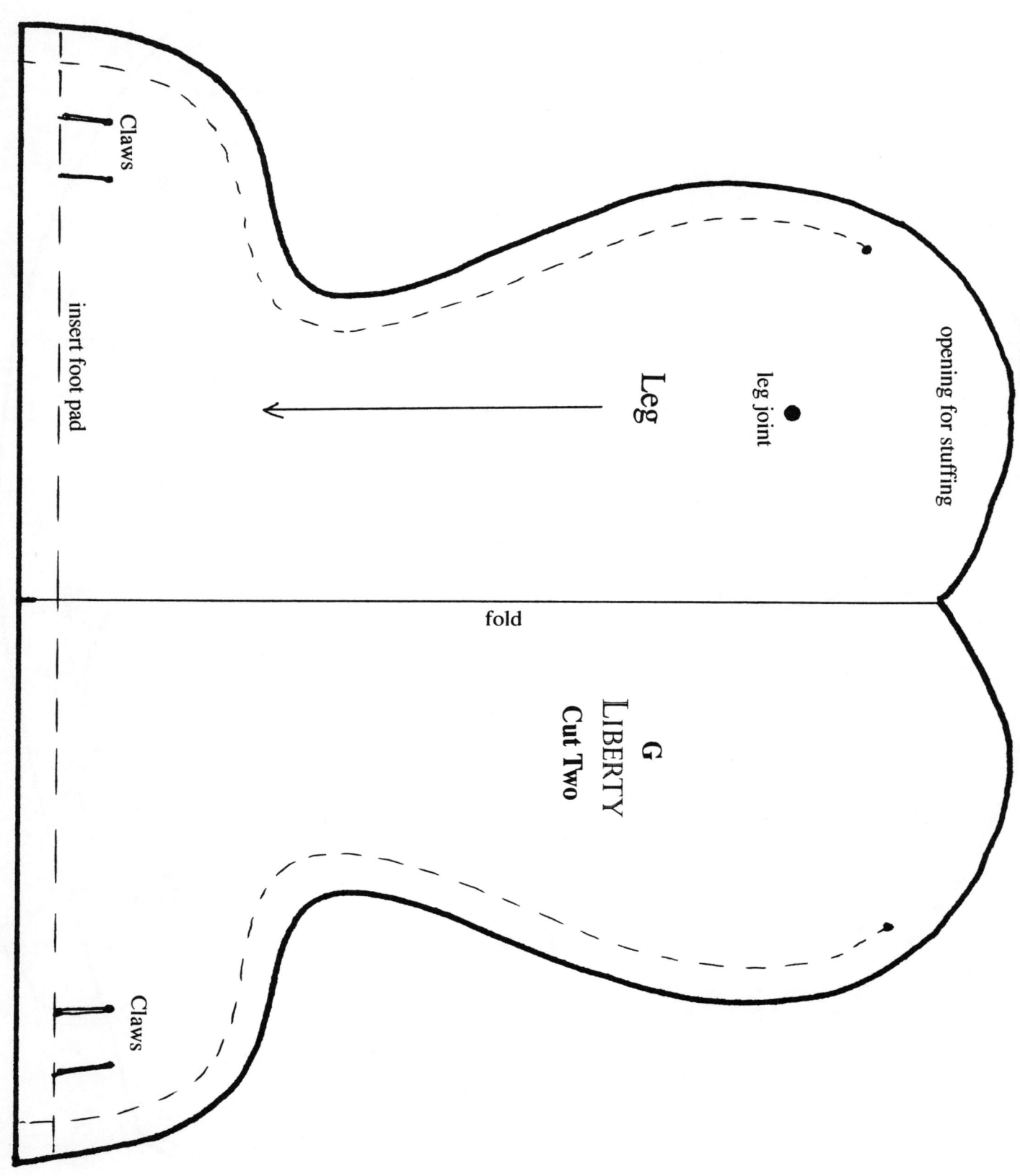

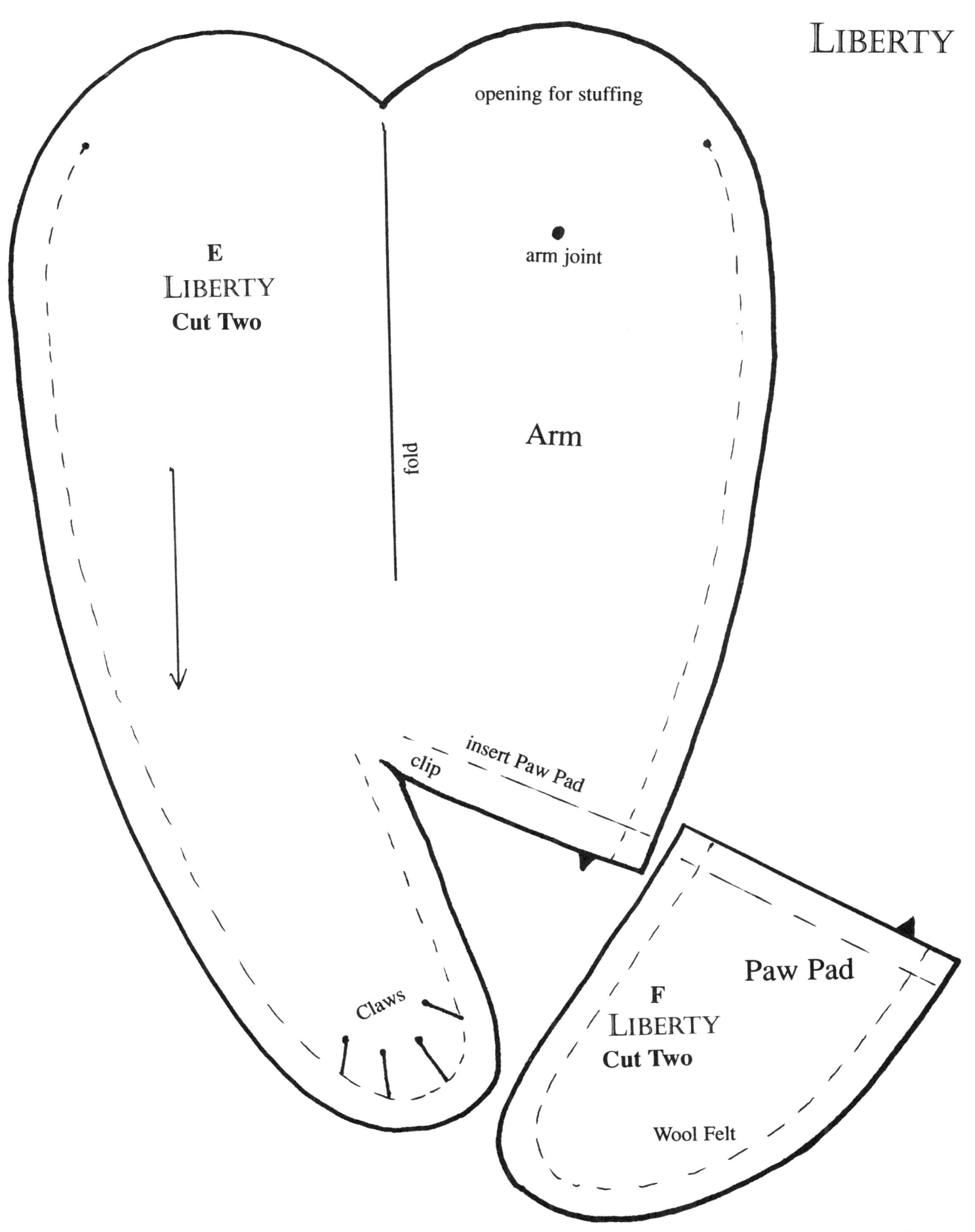

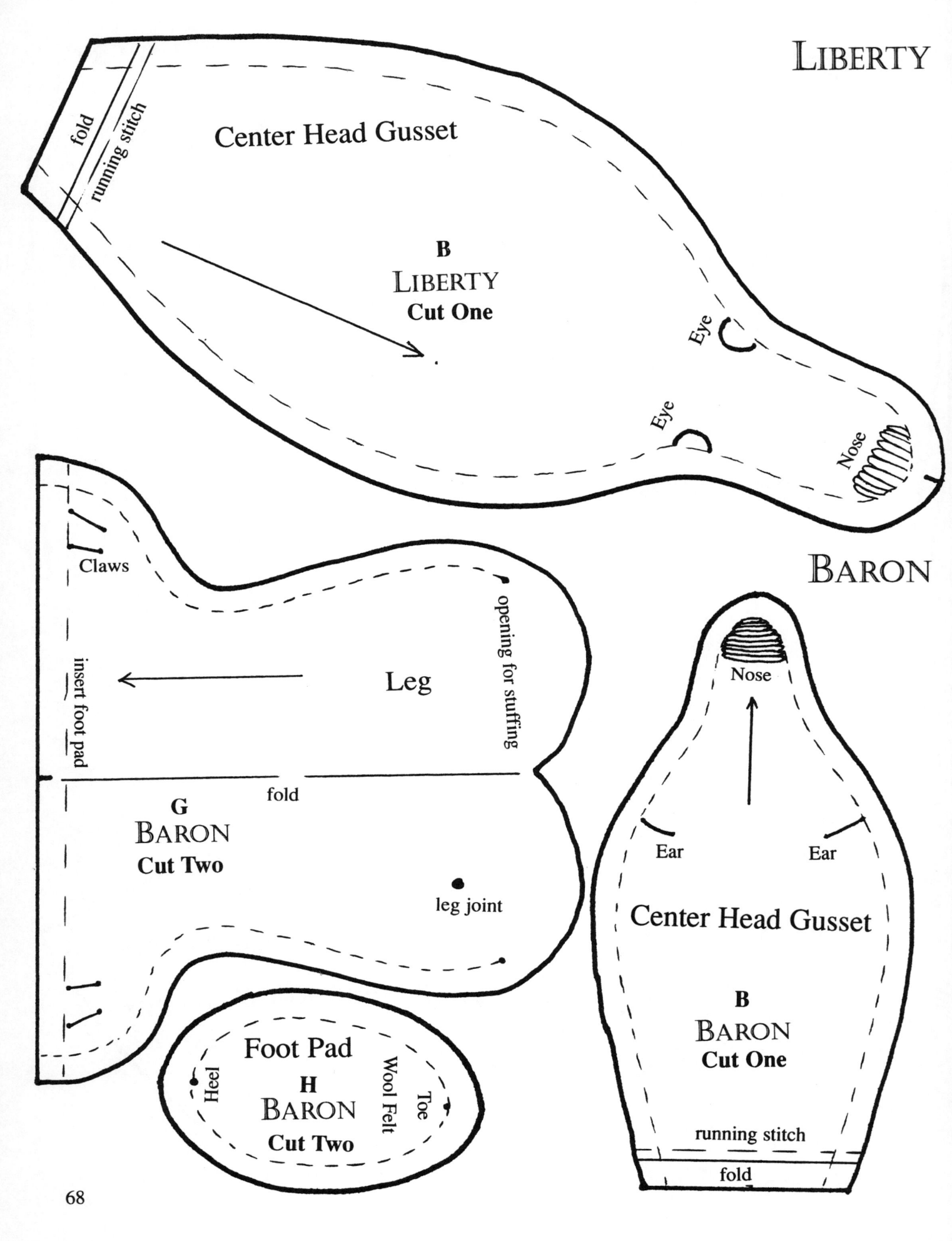

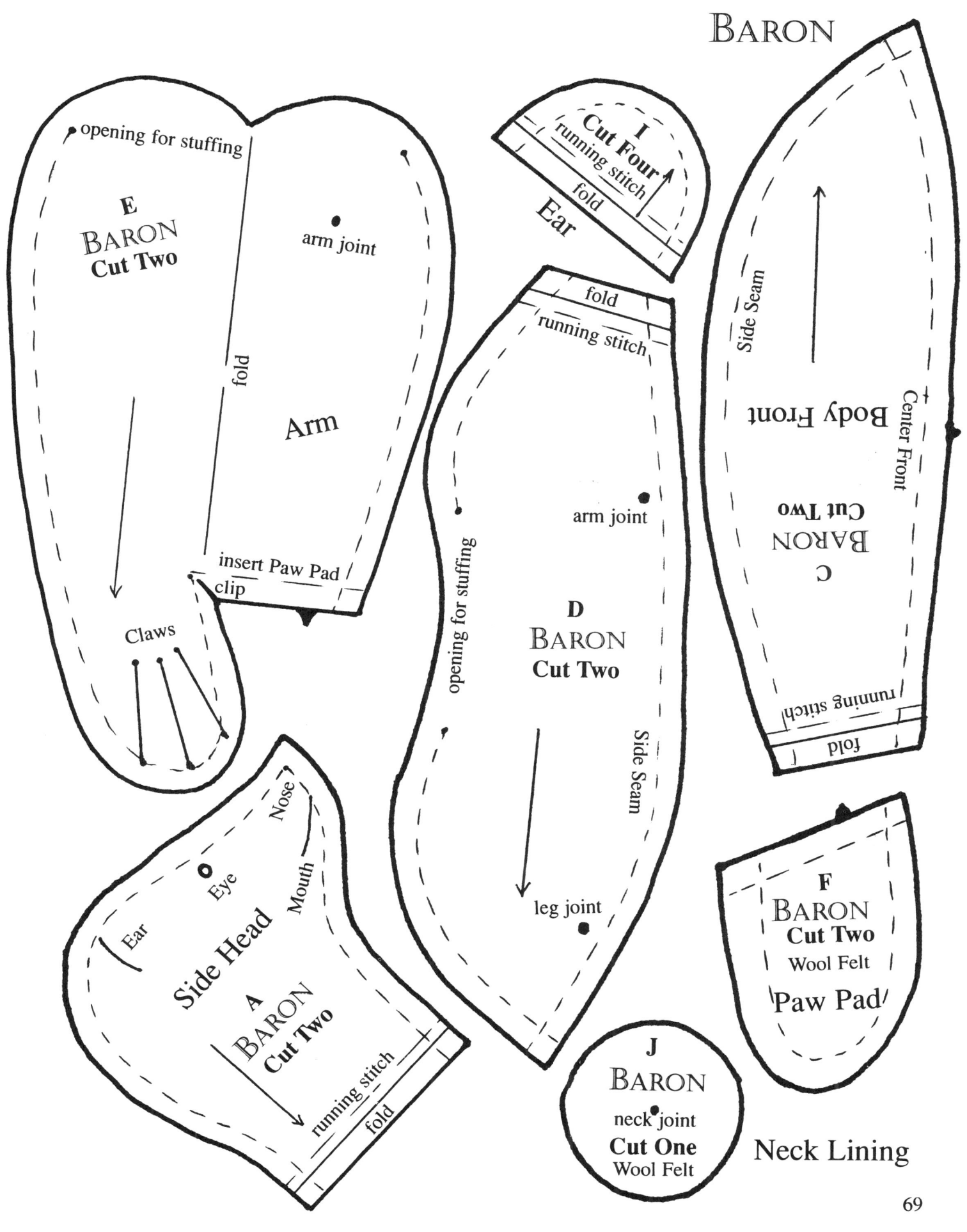

Rolph

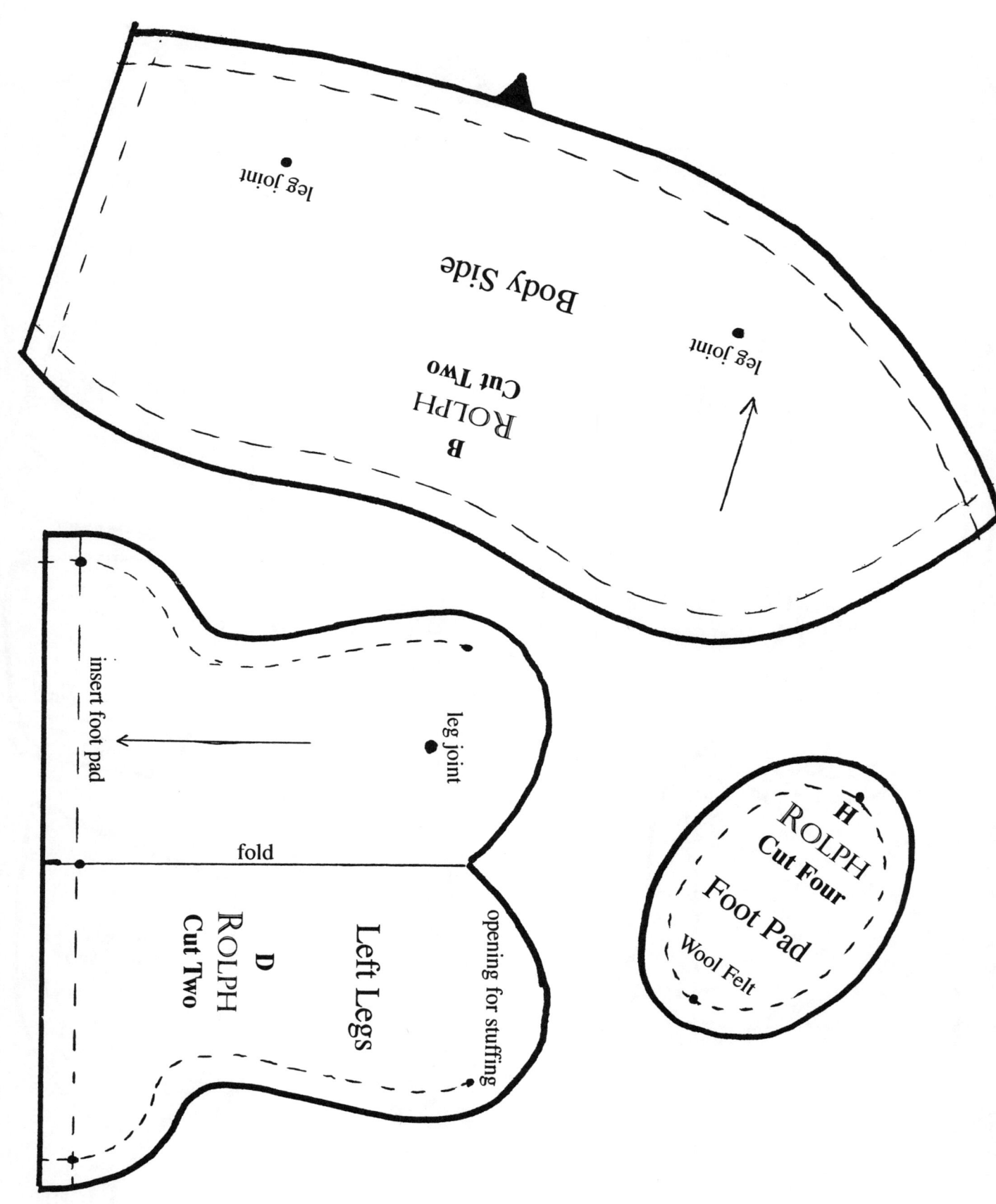

70

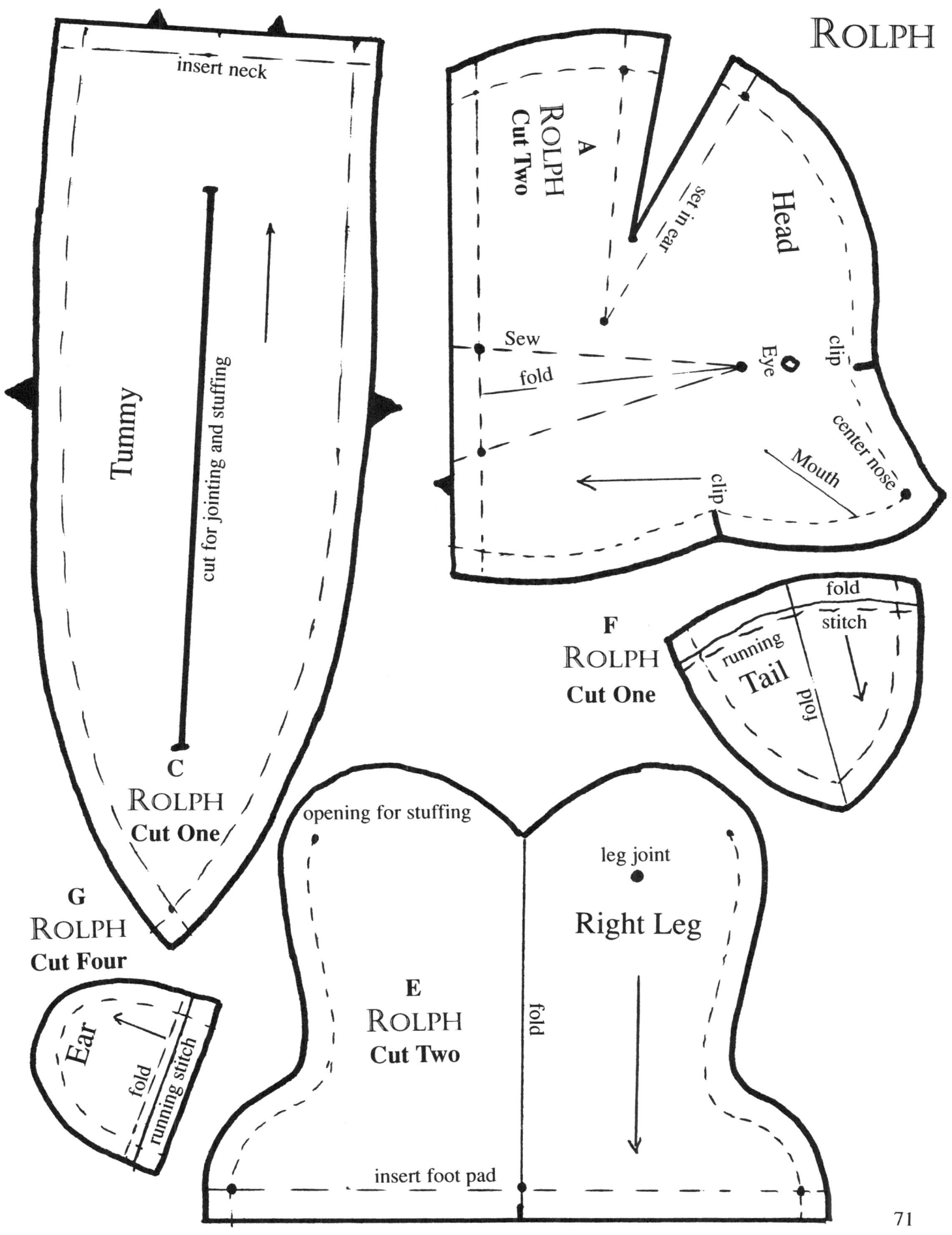

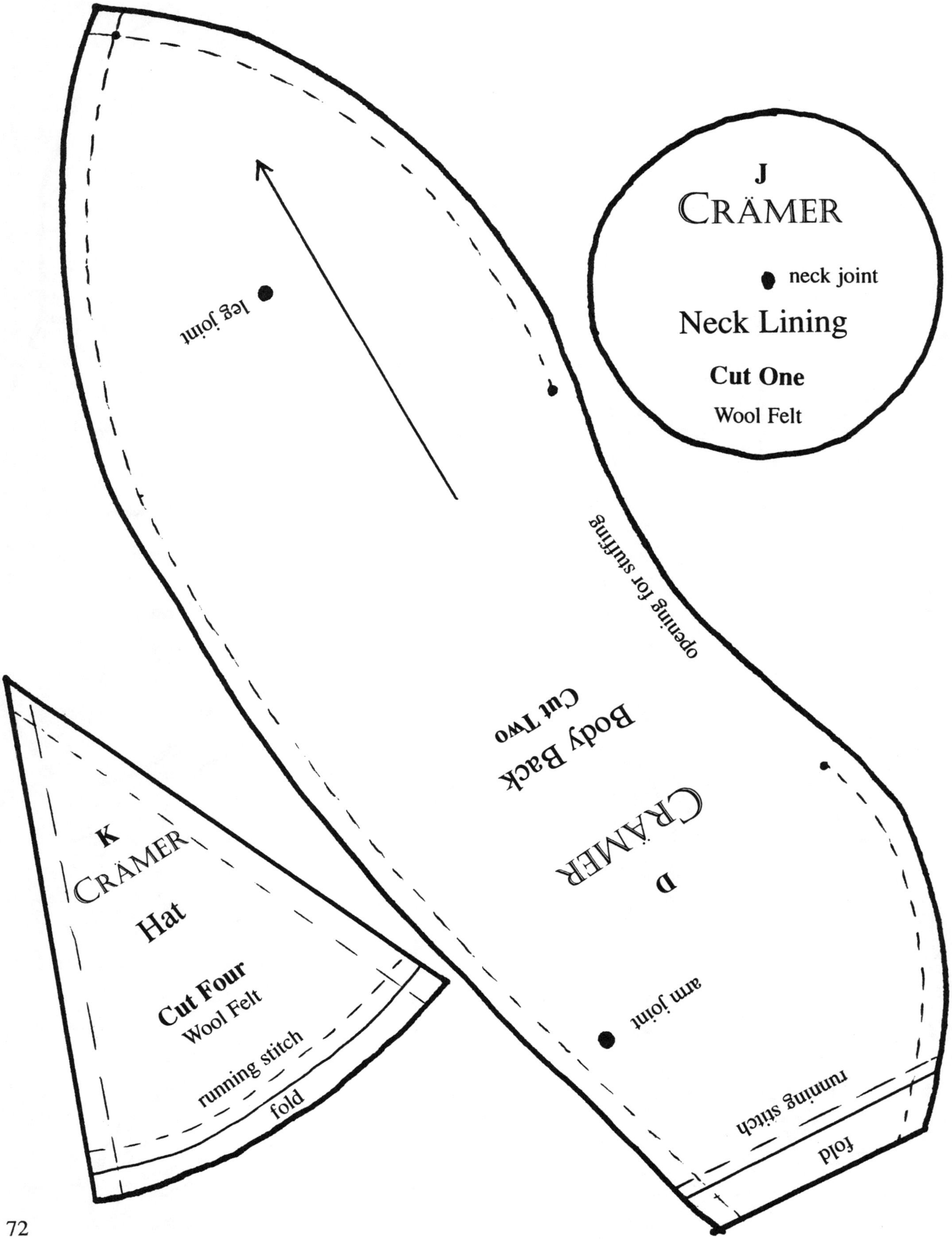

CRÄMER

J
CRÄMER
neck joint
Neck Lining
Cut One
Wool Felt

leg joint

opening for stuffing

D
CRÄMER
Body Back
Cut Two

arm joint

running stitch
fold

K
CRÄMER
Hat
Cut Four
Wool Felt
running stitch
fold

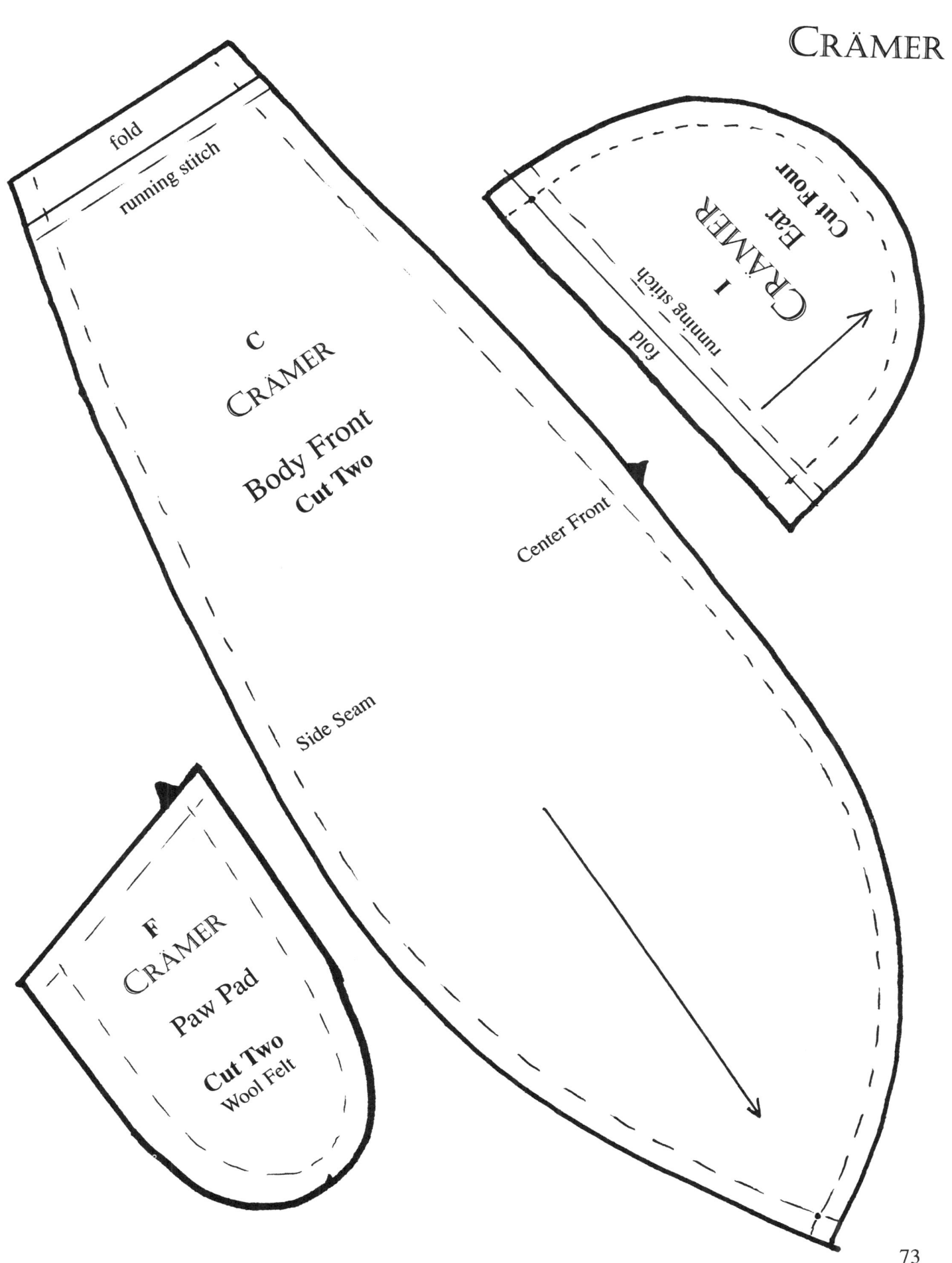

CRÄMER

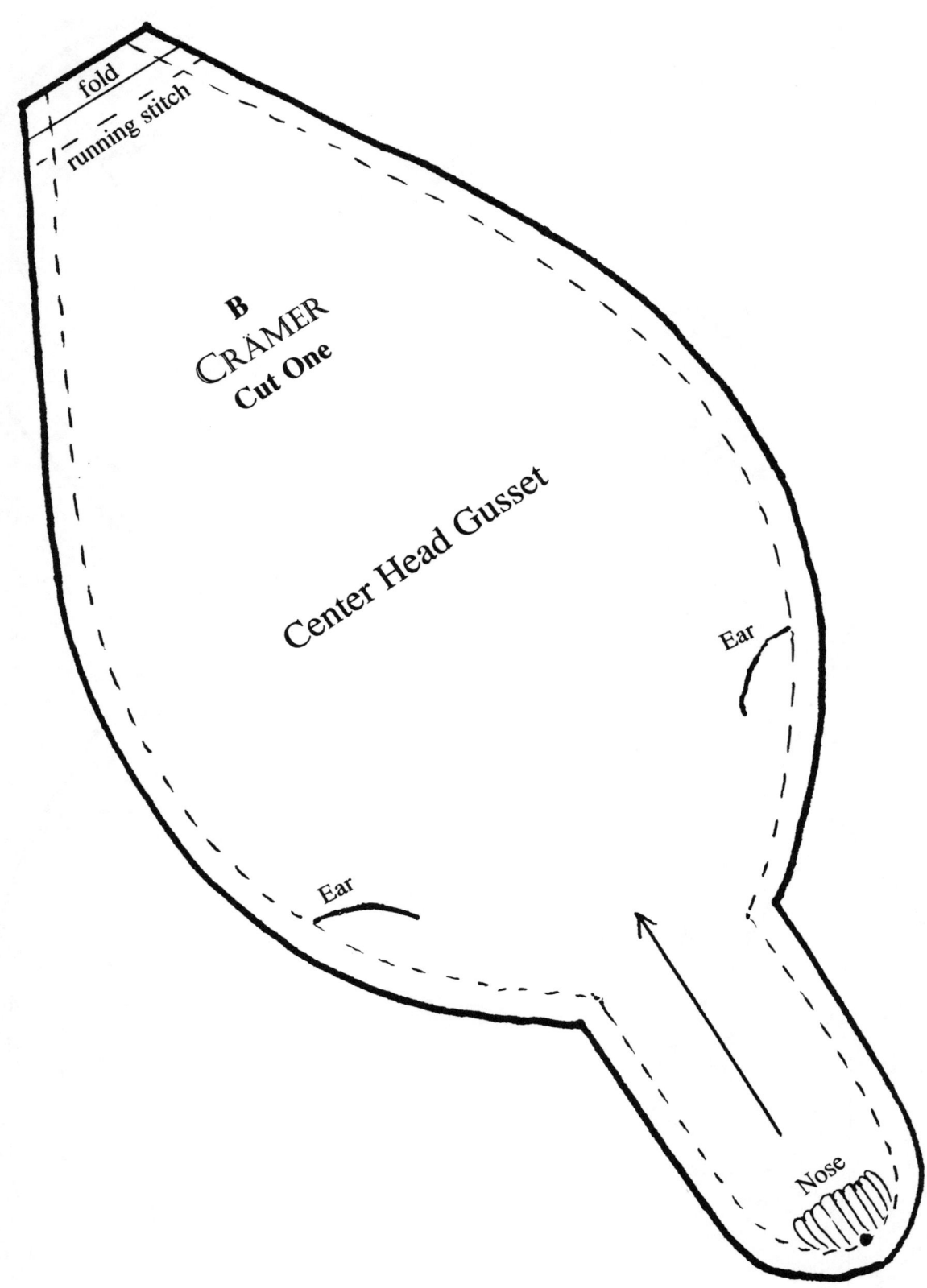

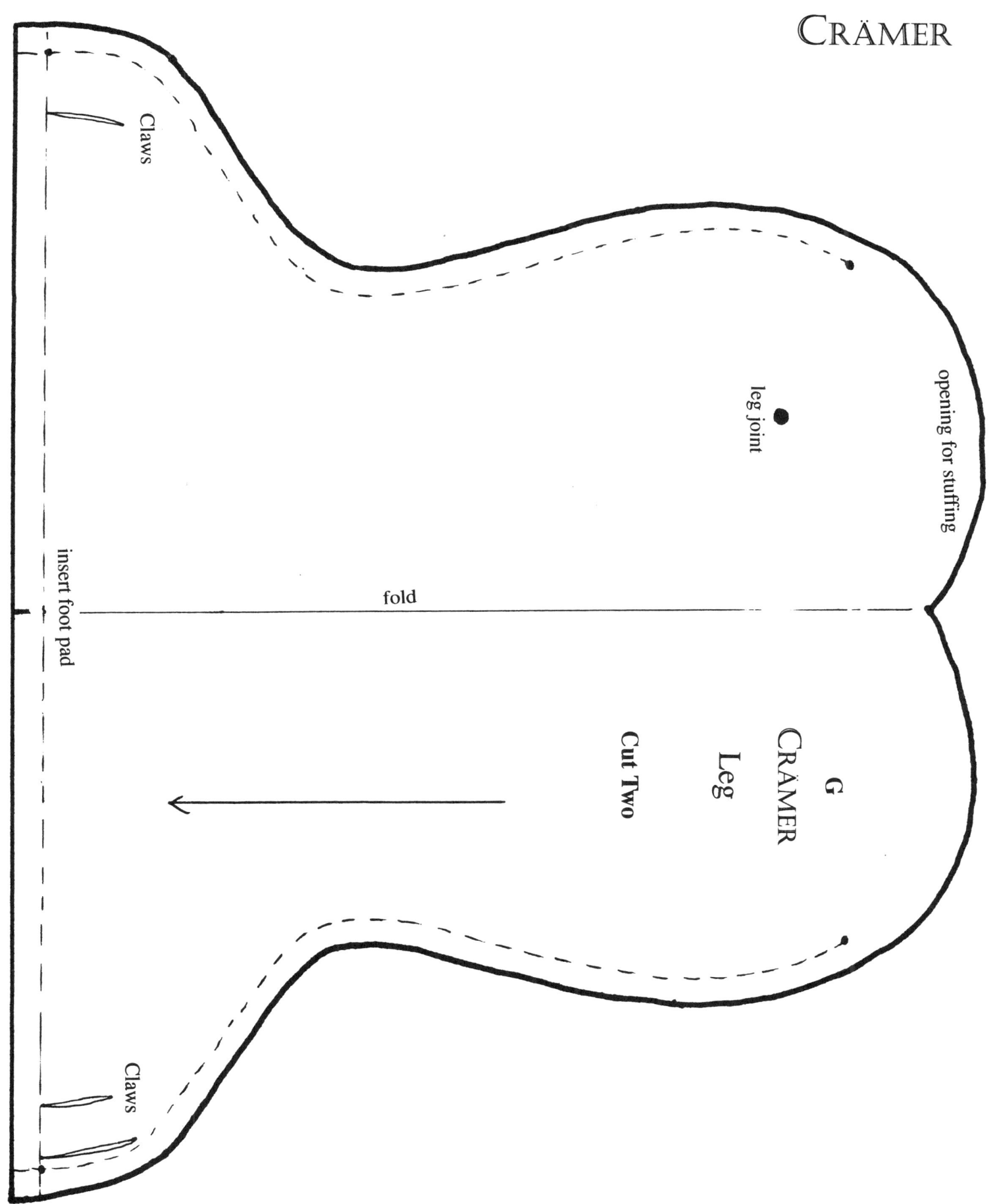

CRÄMER

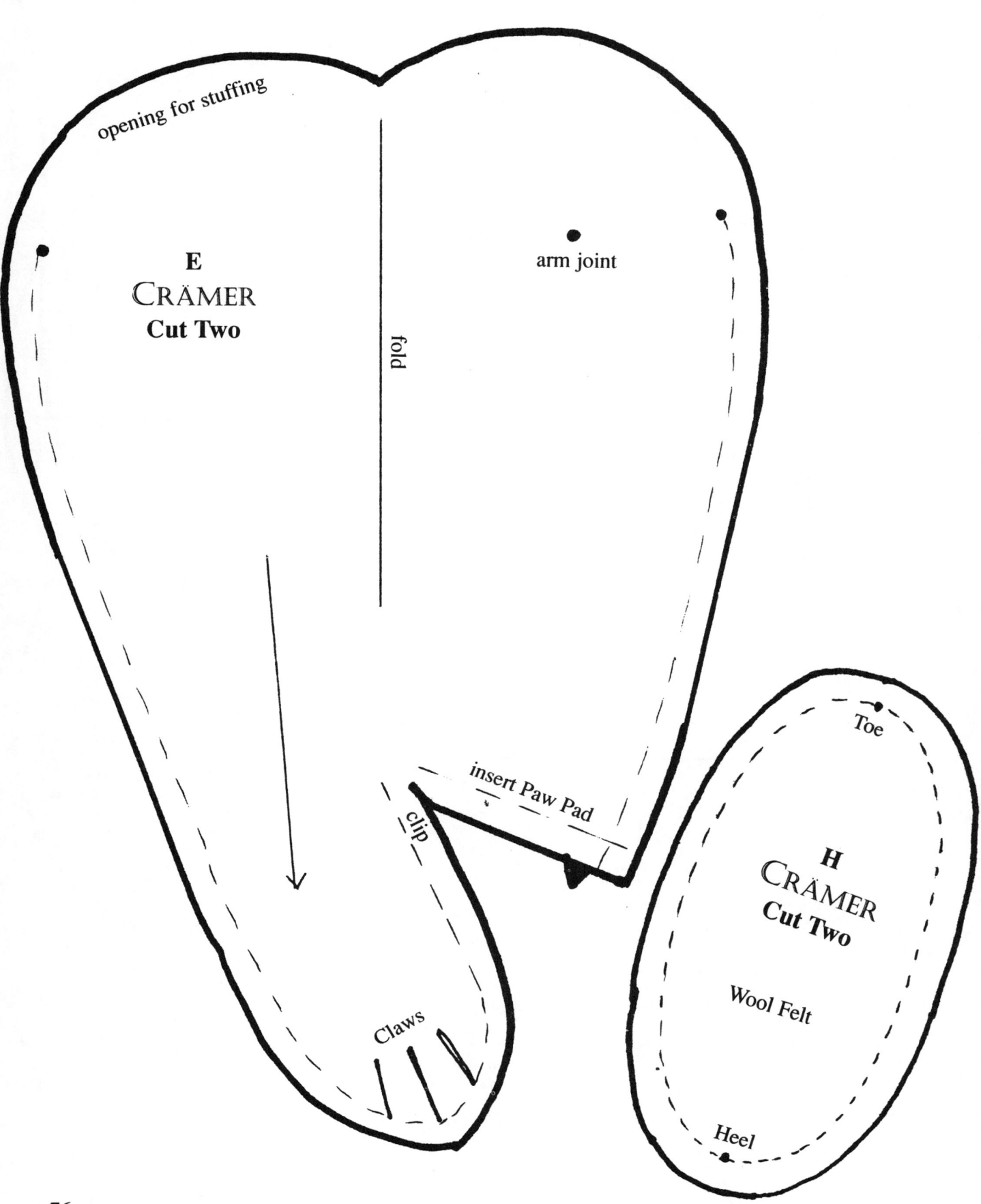

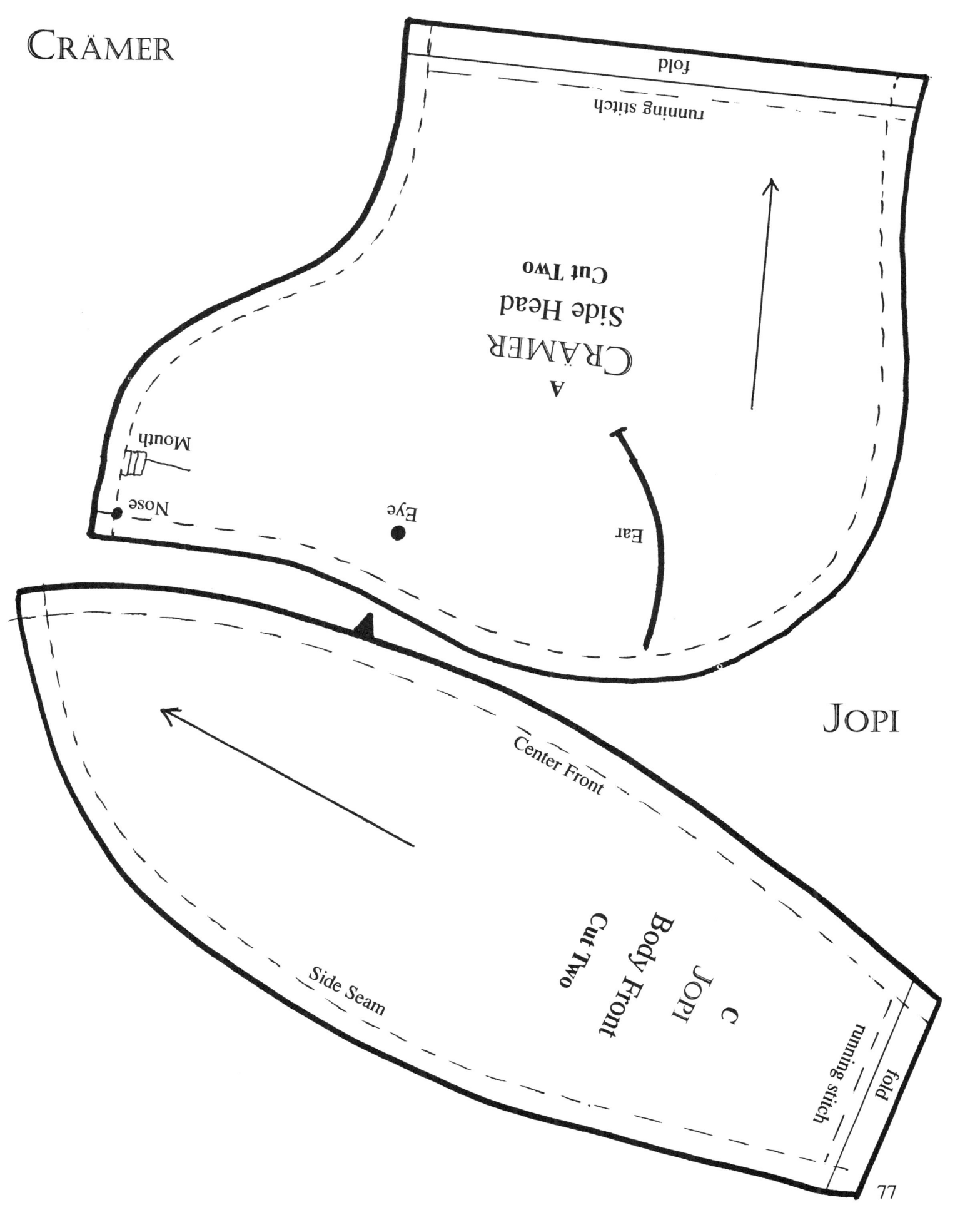

JOPI

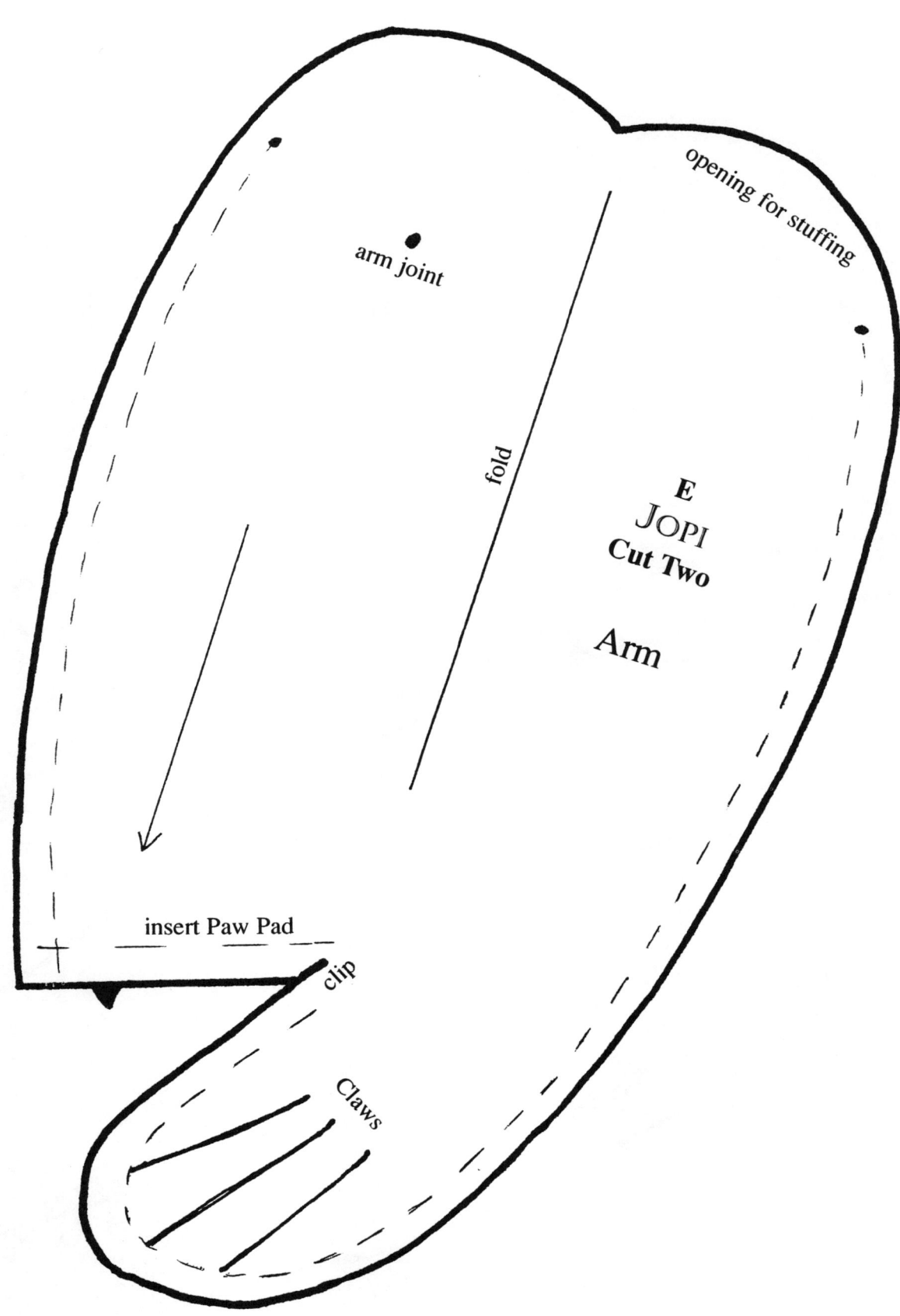

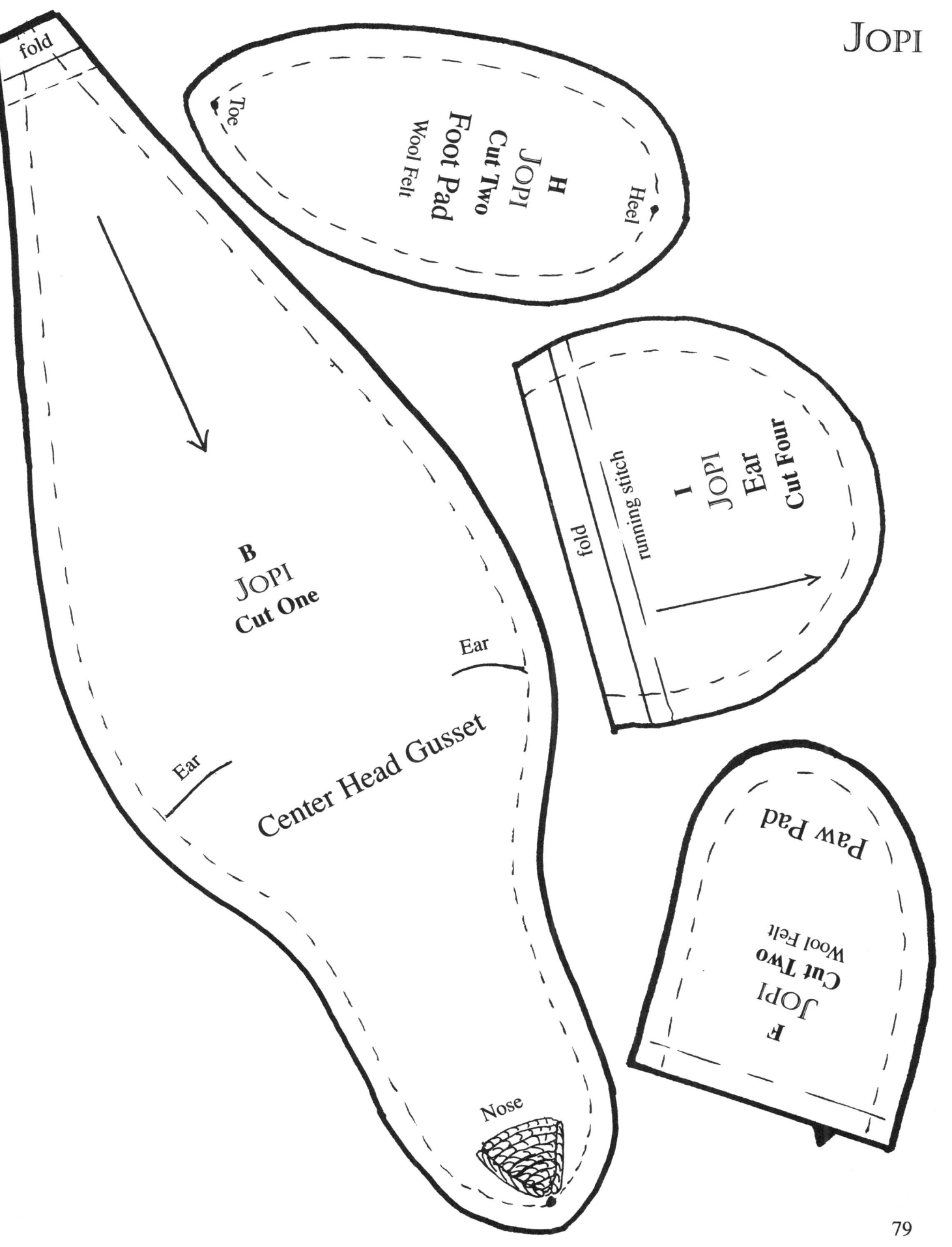

JOPI

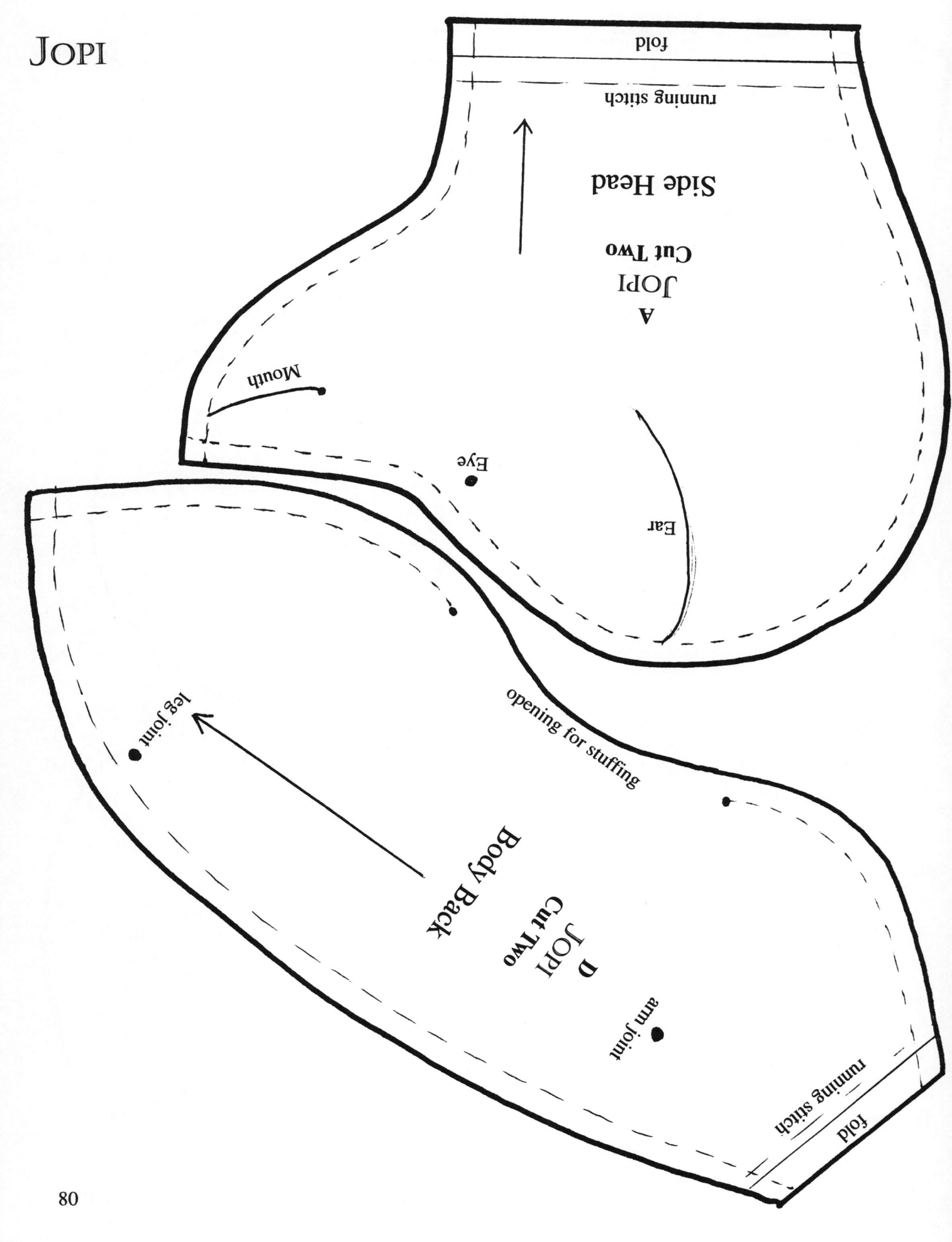

80

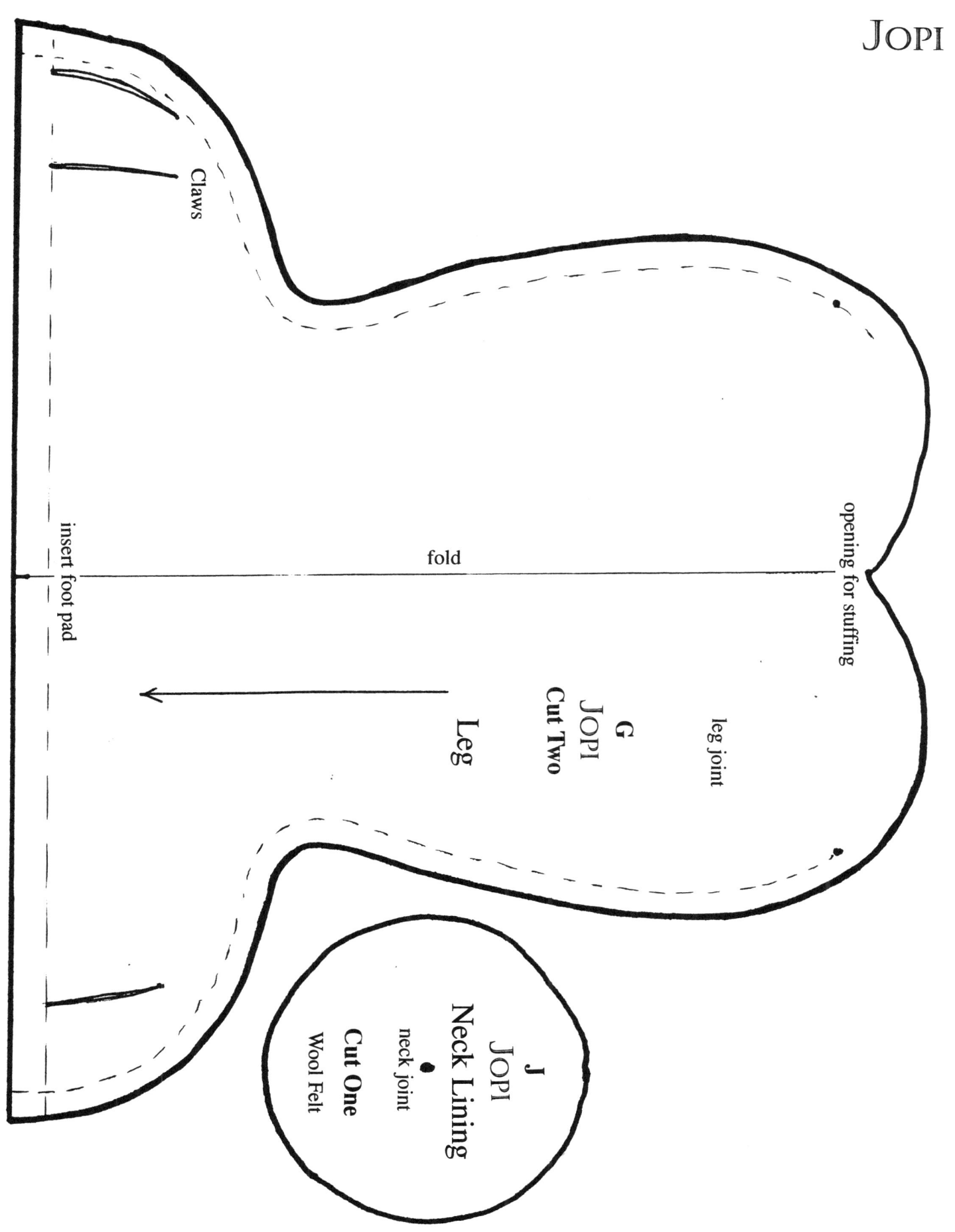

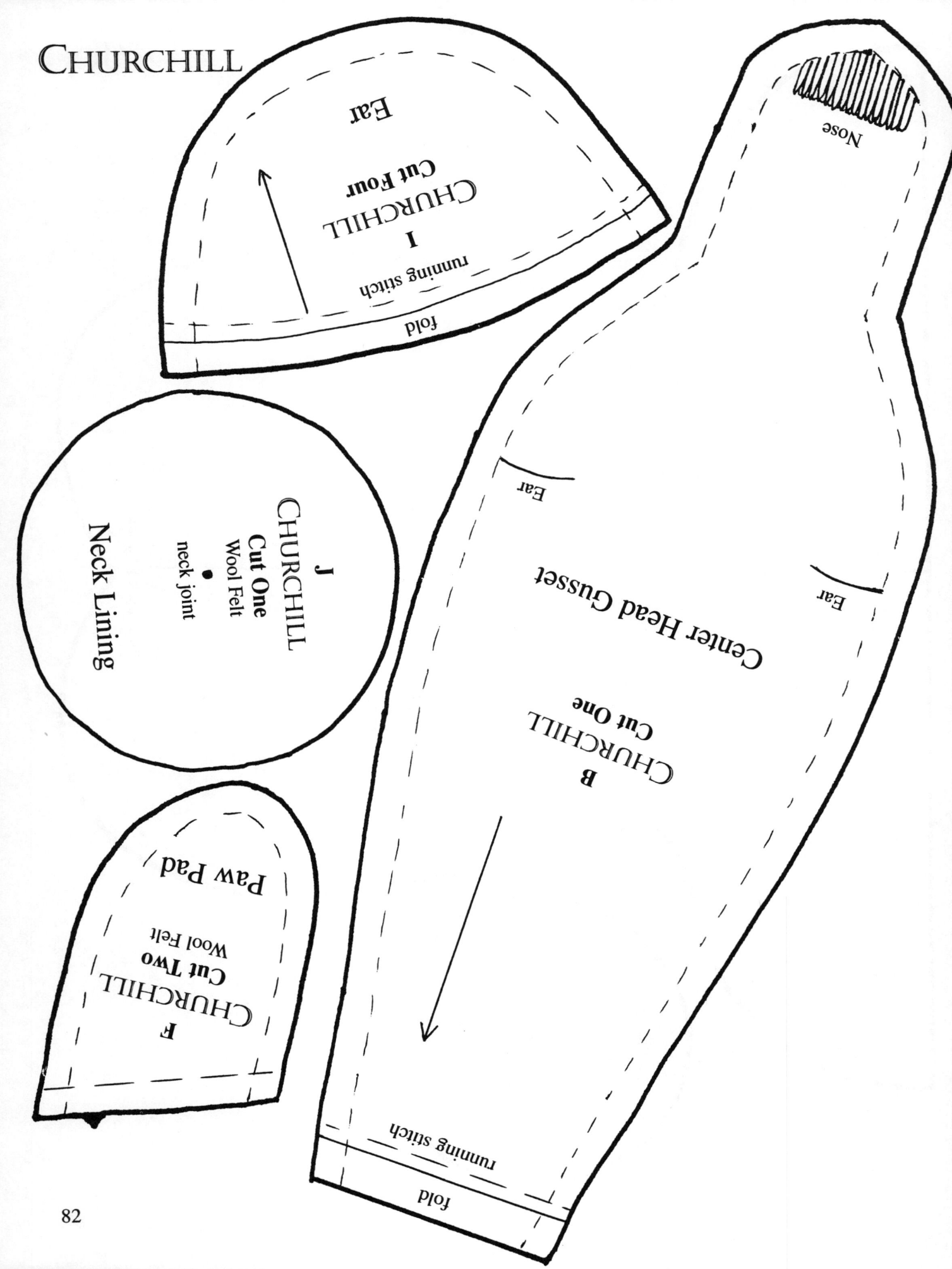

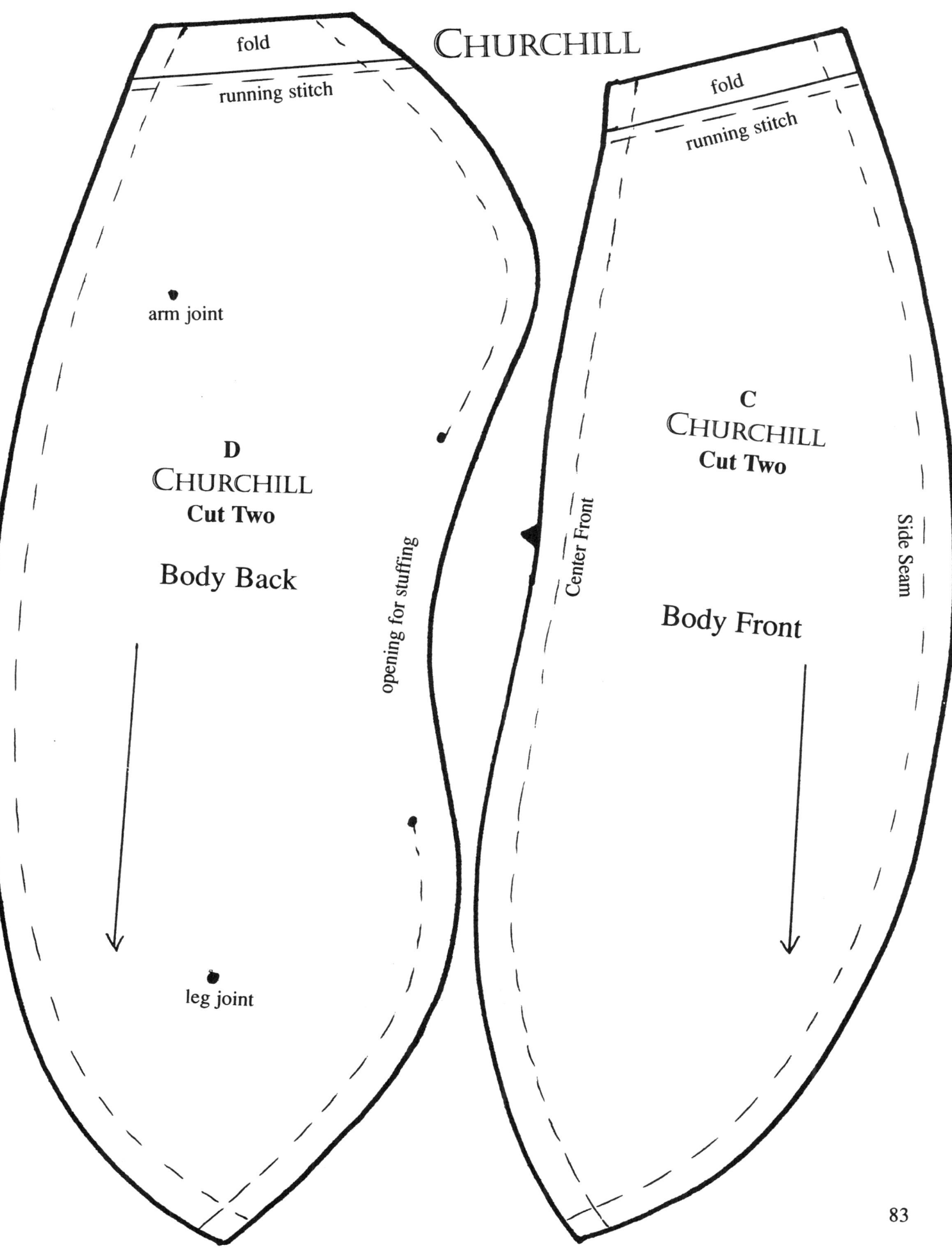

CHURCHILL

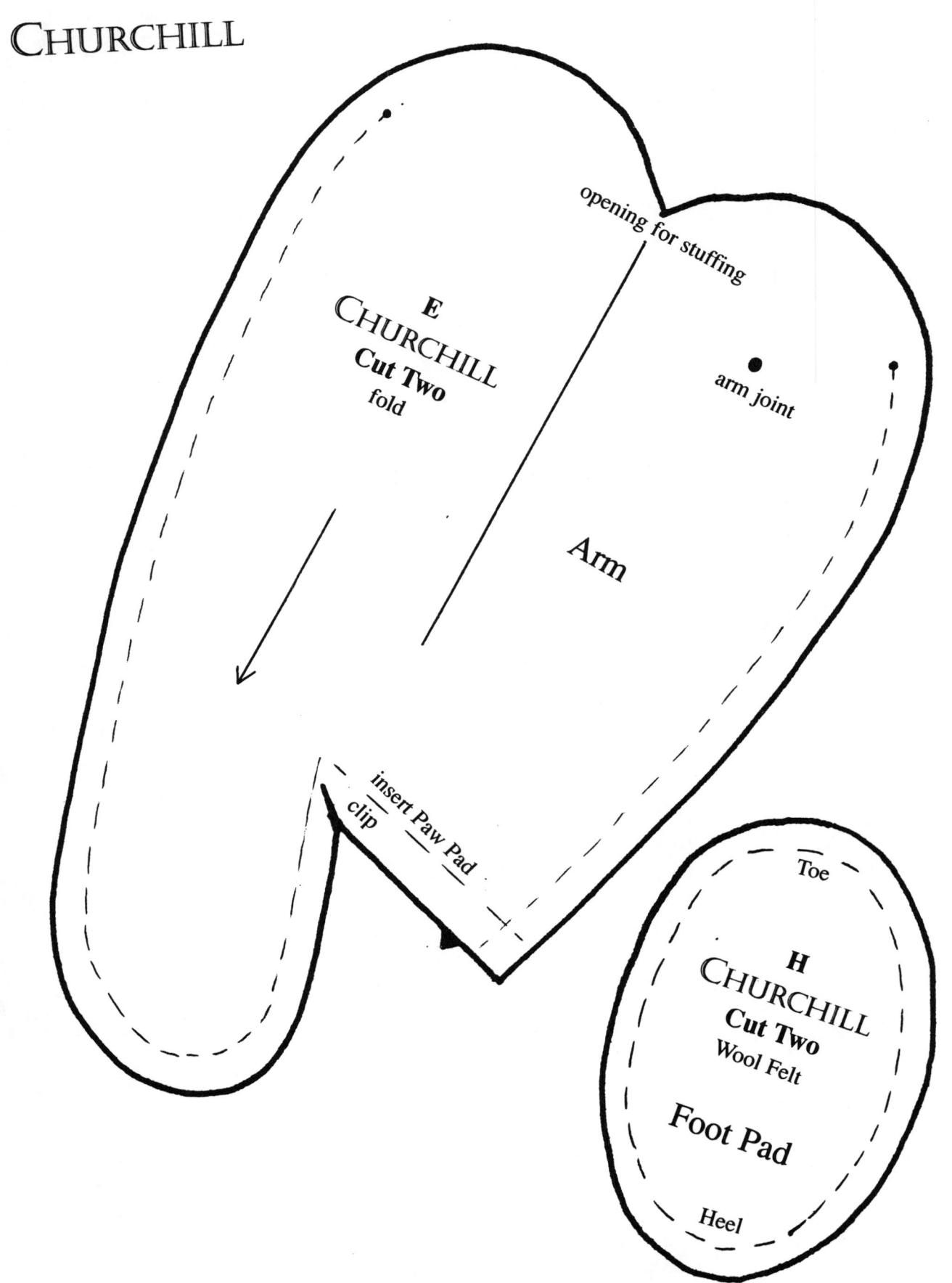

CHURCHILL

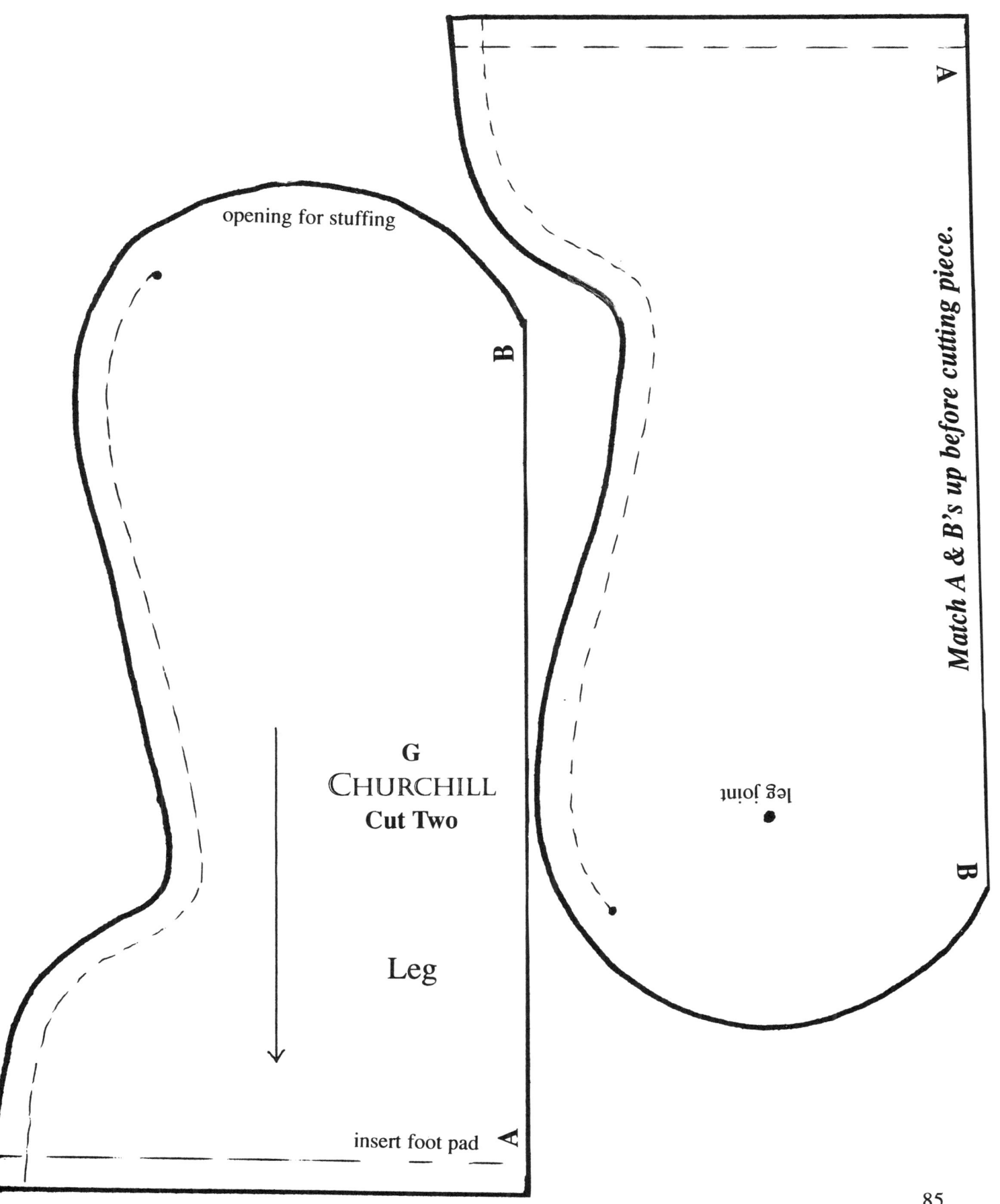

85

Churchill

Chad

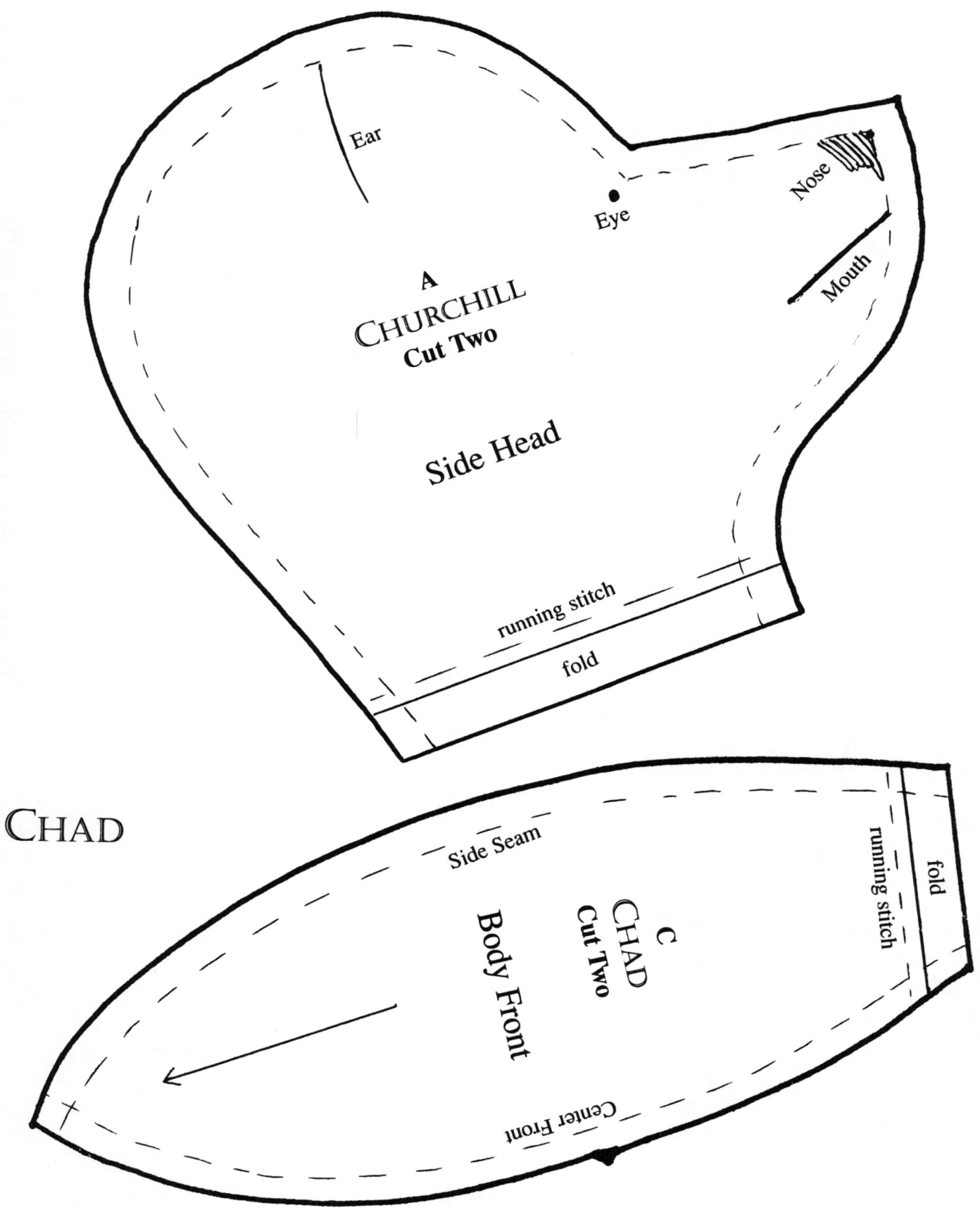

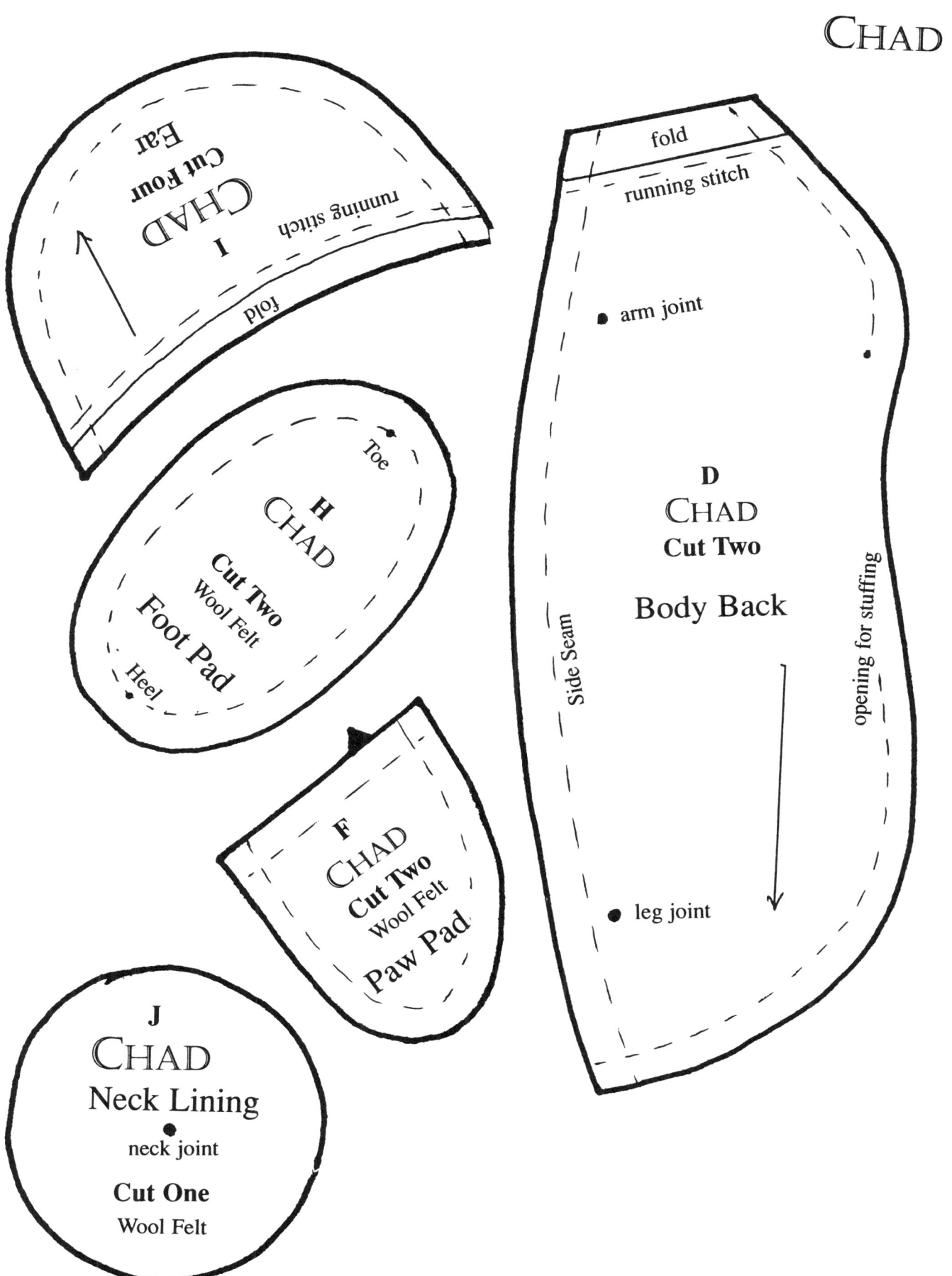

Chad

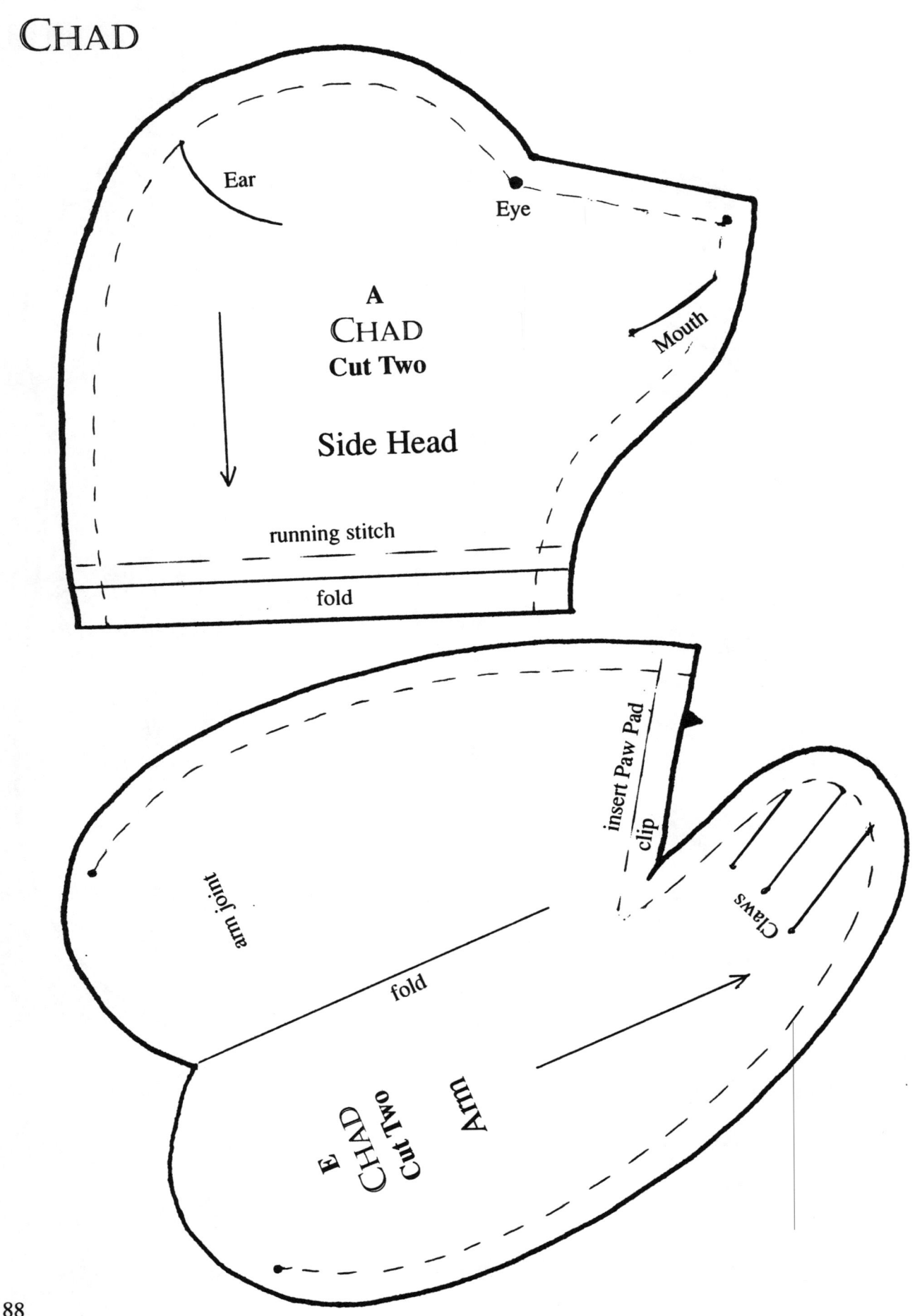

88

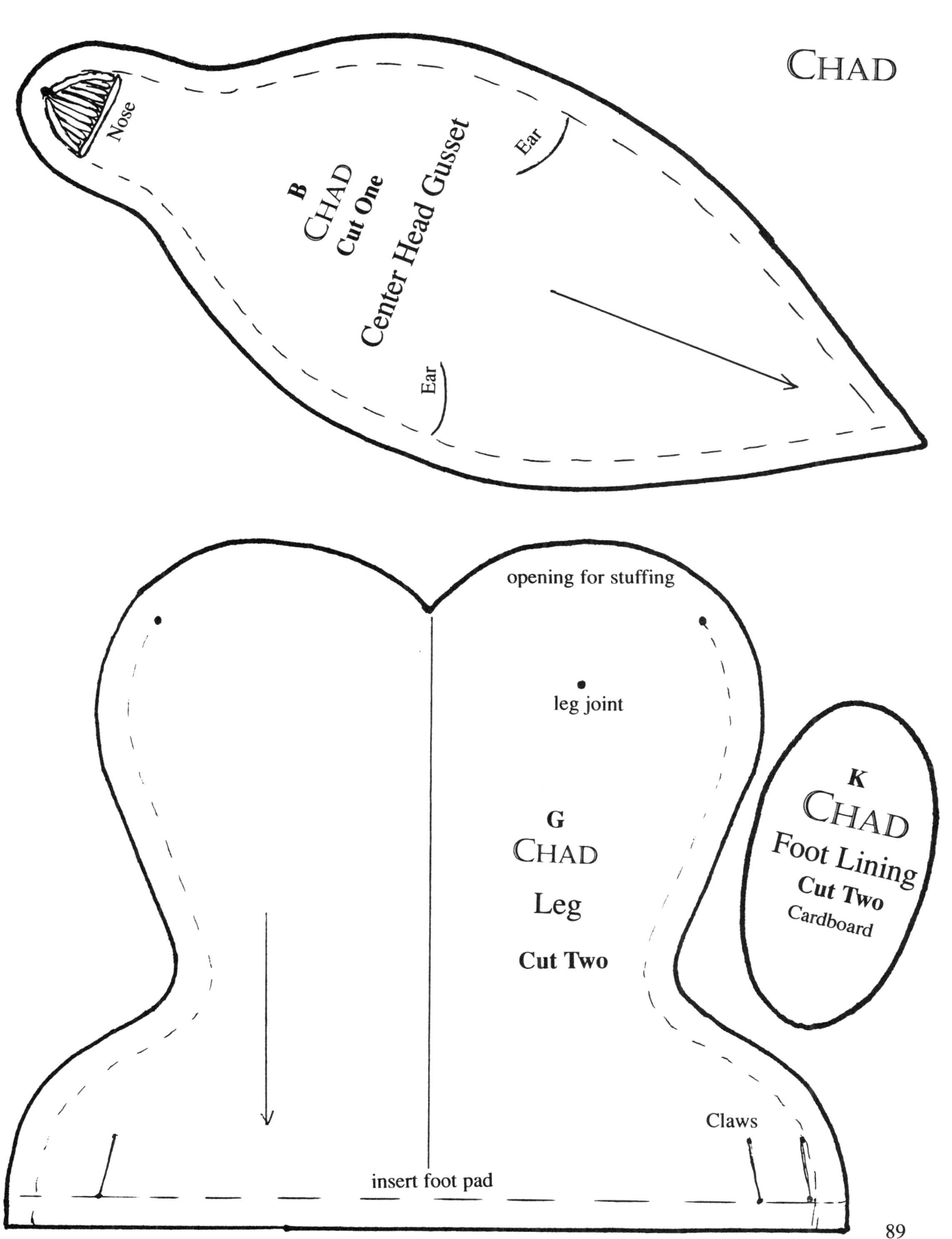

Hangtags

Hangtags

B

Name of Bear: _____
Birthdate: _____
Made By: _____
Proud Parents: _____

© **1995 Linda Mullins**
Artwork by Gisele Nash

A

Name of Bear: _____
Birthdate: _____
Made By: _____
Proud Parents: _____

© **1995 Linda Mullins**
Artwork by Gisele Nash

D

Name of Bear: _____
Birthdate: _____
Made By: _____
Proud Parents: _____

© **1995 Linda Mullins**
Artwork by Gisele Nash

C

Name of Bear: _____
Birthdate: _____
Made By: _____
Proud Parents: _____

© **1995 Linda Mullins**
Artwork by Gisele Nash

Hangtags

Hangtags

F

Name of Bear: _____
Birthdate: _____
Made By: _____
Proud Parents: _____

© 1995 Linda Mullins
Artwork by Gisele Nash

E

Name of Bear: _____
Birthdate: _____
Made By: _____
Proud Parents: _____

© 1995 Linda Mullins
Artwork by Gisele Nash

H

Name of Bear: _____
Birthdate: _____
Made By: _____
Proud Parents: _____

© 1995 Linda Mullins
Artwork by Gisele Nash

G

Name of Bear: _____
Birthdate: _____
Made By: _____
Proud Parents: _____

© 1995 Linda Mullins
Artwork by Gisele Nash

I

Name of Bear: _____
Birthdate: _____
Made By: _____
Proud Parents: _____

© 1995 Linda Mullins
Artwork by Gisele Nash

Other Distinguished Reference Books by
LINDA MULLINS

Linda Mullins is regarded as one of the premier Teddy Bear show promoters in America. She is a leading authority in teddy bear collecting.

AMERICAN TEDDY BEAR ENCYCLOPEDIA
Saluting the American Teddy Bear! From the ritualistic Indian culture focusing on the bear to today's favorite collectible, Linda Mullins presents her extensive research and identification guide to American manufacturing companies such as Gund, Ideal, Knickerbocker, Applause, North American Bear Co., R. John Wright, The Boyds Collection and many more. This book also features one of America's most famous bears - Smokey Bear. The form of the collectible bear is also illustrated with chapters on teddy bear figurines, advertising bears, and teddy bear restoration. A perfect companion to *Tribute to Teddy Bear Artists, American Teddy Bear Encyclopedia* is your encyclopedia to American Teddies! 140 color of 300 photos. 144 pages. 8-1/2" x 11". HB. Item #H4852. $29.95

TEDDY BEAR ARTISTS POSTCARDS
Discover the magic of the artist made teddy bear through 30 distinctive ready-to-use postcards. Colorful photographs capture the teddy's spirit and personality. Compilation of today's American and international artists. Buy two, one to use - one to save or collect. 6-3/8" x 4-1/4". PB. Item #H4862. $6.95

TRIBUTE TO TEDDY BEAR ARTISTS
What is teddy bear art? Who are teddy bear artists? Discover the myriad of answers through the personal accounts of 130 popular teddy bear artists from around the world. These artists are members of an elite fraternity of creative people who are able to express unique feelings with unprecedented freshness and vitality. They share their woes and joys in personal accounts of their very first bear creations as well as sharing bear making tips ranging from easy nose designing to correct fur stitching. Learn these tricks of the trade and ways to market your own bear creations from their expertise! 160 pages. 300 photos. 8-1/2" x 11". HB. Item #H4742. $29.95

4TH TEDDY BEAR & FRIENDS® PRICE GUIDE
Latest values on bears, rabbits, cats and dogs as well as a wealth of other animals are featured! This book shows and values what is being collected today! Such important collectibles as Muffy, antique, collectible, manufacturer and artist are featured as well as a large section devoted to such popular companies as Steiff, North American Bear, Gund and limited editions from Steiff Museum Collection. Charts as well as 358 stunning photographs capturing the character of bears and their friends. 176 pages. 118 color photos. 6" x 9". PB. Item #H4438. $12.95

TEDDY BEARS PAST & PRESENT, VOLUME I
Regarded as THE COLLECTOR'S IDENTIFICATION GUIDE, this volume contains a wealth of critical background information on the history of leading bear manufacturers and over 600 photographs, 80 in color, of the bears they produced. *Teddy Bears Past & Present* makes it easy to determine the price of your favorite bears because of its visual and chronological order. Best presentation about the distinguishing characteristics of bears, labels and tags. 304 pages. 8-1/2" x 11". HB. Item #H3120. $29.95

TEDDY BEARS PAST & PRESENT, VOLUME II
As the companion to Volume I, *Teddy Bears Past & Present, II* provides more in depth research into the gems of the history of the teddy bear. This research includes such diverse topics as today's bruin collecting and manufacturing in Germany, America, Britain, Australia, Japan and France as well as biographies of elite teddy bear artists and a wealth of photographs of their bears. Over 500 photos, 153 in stunning full-color. 304 pages. 8-1/2" x 11". HB. Item #H4330. $25.00

THE RAIKES BEAR & DOLL STORY (*Revised Edition*)
Revised values with many new photos. Robert Raikes fans have something new to cheer about! An exquisite photograph album and very readable story of how Raikes' phenomenal bears came to be and their evolution into one of the hottest bear collectibles ever. Includes fascinating photos of the early carvings through the bears and dolls produced in 1993 as well as some exquisite one-of-a-kind pieces. 120 pages. 250 photographs, 167 in color! 8-1/2" x 11". HB. Item #H4654 $22.95